THE YOGA AND ITS OBJECTS

SRI AUROBINDO

THE YOGA AND ITS OBJECTS

SRI AUROBINDO ASHRAM
PUDUCHERRY

First edition 1921
Eleventh edition 2002
Third impression 2012

Rs 28
ISBN 978-81-7058-677-7

Published by Sri Aurobindo Ashram Publication Department
Pondicherry 605 002
Web http://www.sabda.in

Printed at Sri Aurobindo Ashram Press, Pondicherry
PRINTED IN INDIA

Publisher's Note

This essay, which is mentioned in a letter written by Sri Aurobindo in 1912, was first published as a booklet in 1921 under the title "The Yoga and Its Object". The title was changed to the present form in the second edition, issued in 1922. New editions were published in 1931, 1938, 1943, 1946, 1949 and subsequently. In 1934 Sri Aurobindo wrote that the booklet represented "an early stage" of his sadhana "and only a part of it is applicable to the Yoga as it has at present taken form after a lapse of more than twenty years". The Appendix consists of explanations of certain words and phrases in the essay, written by Sri Aurobindo in June 1938 in answer to questions posed by a disciple.

The Yoga and Its Objects

The yoga we practise is not for ourselves alone, but for the Divine; its aim is to work out the will of the Divine in the world, to effect a spiritual transformation and to bring down a divine nature and a divine life into the mental, vital and physical nature and life of humanity. Its object is not personal Mukti, although Mukti is a necessary condition of the yoga, but the liberation and transformation of the human being. It is not personal Ananda, but the bringing down of the divine Ananda — Christ's kingdom of heaven, our Satyayuga — upon the earth. Of *mokṣa* we have no personal need; for the soul is *nityamukta* and bondage is an illusion. We play at being bound, we are not really bound. We can be free when God wills; for he, our supreme Self, is the master of the game, and without his grace and permission no soul can leave the game. It is often God's will in us to take through the mind the *bhoga* of ignorance, of the dualities, of joy and grief, of pleasure and pain, of virtue and sin, of enjoyment and renunciation: for long ages, in many countries, he never even thinks of the yoga but plays out this play century after century without wearying of it. There is nothing evil in this, nothing which we need condemn or from which we need shrink, — it is God's play. The wise man is he who recognises this truth and knowing his freedom, yet plays out God's play, waiting for his command to change the methods of the game.

The command is now. God always keeps for himself a

chosen country in which the higher knowledge is through all chances and dangers, by the few or the many, continually preserved, and for the present, in this Chaturyuga at least, that country is India. Whenever he chooses to take the full pleasure of ignorance, of the dualities, of strife and wrath and tears and weakness and selfishness, the tamasic and rajasic pleasures, of the play of the Kali in short, he dims the knowledge in India and puts her down into weakness and degradation so that she may retire into herself and not interfere with this movement of his Lila. When he wants to rise up from the mud and Narayana in man to become once again mighty and wise and blissful, then he once more pours out the knowledge on India and raises her up so that she may give the knowledge with its necessary consequences of might, wisdom and bliss to the whole world. When there is the contracted movement of knowledge, the yogins in India withdraw from the world and practise yoga for their own liberation and delight or for the liberation of a few disciples; but when the movement of knowledge again expands and the soul of India expands with it, they come forth once more and work in the world and for the world. Yogins like Janaka, Ajatashatru and Kartavirya once more sit on the thrones of the world and govern the nations.

God's Lila in man moves always in a circle, from Satyayuga to Kali and through Kali to the Satya, from the Age of Gold to the Age of Iron and back again through the Iron to the Gold. In modern language the Satyayuga is a period of the world in which a harmony, stable and sufficient, is created and man realises for a time, under certain conditions and limitations, the perfection of his being. The harmony exists in its nature, by the force of a settled purity; but afterwards it begins to break down and man upholds it, in the Treta, by force of will, individual and collective; it breaks down further and he attempts to uphold it in the Dwapara by intellectual regulation and common consent and rule; then in the Kali it finally collapses and is destroyed. But the Kali is not merely evil; in it the necessary conditions are progressively built up for a new Satya, another harmony, a more advanced perfection. In the period of the Kali which has passed, still endures in its effects, but is now at an end, there has been a general destruction of the ancient knowledge and culture. Only a few fragments remain to us in the Vedas, Upanishads and other sacred works and in the world's confused traditions. But the time is at hand for a first movement upward, the first attempt to build up a new harmony and perfection. That is the reason why so many ideas are abroad for the perfection of human society, knowledge, religion and morals. But the true harmony has not yet been found.

It is only India that can discover the harmony, because it is only by a change — not a mere readjustment — of man's present nature that it can be developed, and such a change is not possible except by yoga. The nature of man and of things is at present a discord, a harmony that has got out of tune. The whole heart and action and mind of man must be changed, but from within, not from without, not by political and social institutions, not even by creeds and philosophies, but by realisation of God in ourselves and the world and a remoulding of life by that realisation. This can only be effected by Purnayoga, a yoga not devoted to a particular purpose, even though that purpose be Mukti or Ananda, but to the fulfilment of the divine humanity in ourselves and others. For this purpose the practices of Hatha and Raja Yoga are not sufficient and even the Trimarga will not serve; we must go higher and resort to the Adhyatmayoga. The principle of Adhyatmayoga is, in knowledge, the realisation of all things that we see or do not see but are aware of, — men, things, ourselves, events, gods, titans, angels, — as one divine Brahman, and in action and attitude, an absolute self-surrender to the Paratpara Purusha, the transcendent, infinite and universal Personality who is at once personal and impersonal, finite and infinite, self-limiting and illimitable, one and many, and informs with his being not only the Gods above, but man and the worm and the clod below. The surrender must be complete. Nothing must be reserved, no desire, no demand, no opinion, no idea that this must be, that cannot be, that this should be and that should not be; — all must be given. The heart must be purified of all desire, the intellect of all self-will, every duality must be renounced, the whole world seen and unseen must be recognised as one supreme expression of concealed Wisdom, Power and Bliss, and the entire being given up, as an engine is passive in the hands of the driver, for the divine Love, Might and perfect Intelligence to do its work and fulfil its divine Lila. *Ahaṅkāra* must be blotted out in order that we may have, as God intends us ultimately to have, the perfect bliss, the perfect calm and knowledge and the perfect activity of the divine existence. If this attitude of perfect self-surrender can be even imperfectly established, all necessity of Yogic *kriyā* inevitably ceases. For then God himself in us becomes the sadhaka and the siddha and his divine power works in us, not by our artificial processes, but by a working of Nature which is perfectly informed, all-searching and infallibly efficient. Even the most powerful Rajayogic *saṁyama*, the most developed *prāṇāyāma*, the most strenuous meditation, the most ecstatic Bhakti, the most self-denying action, mighty as they are and efficacious, are comparatively weak in their results when set beside this supreme working. For those are all limited to a certain extent by our capacity, but this is illimitable in potency because it is God's capacity. It is only limited by his will which knows what is best for the world and for each of us in the world and apart from it.

The first process of the yoga is to make the *saṅkalpa* of *ātmasamarpaṇa*. Put yourself with all your heart and all your strength into God's hands. Make no conditions, ask for nothing, not even for *siddhi* in the yoga, for nothing at all except that in you and through you his will may be directly performed. To those who demand from him, God gives what they demand, but to those who give themselves and demand nothing, he gives everything that they might otherwise have asked or needed and in addition he gives himself and the spontaneous boons of his love.

The next process is to stand aside and watch the working of the divine power in yourself. This working is often attended with disturbance and trouble in the system, therefore faith is necessary, though perfect faith is not always possible at once; for whatever impurity is in you, harboured openly or secretly lurking, is likely to rise at first and be repeated so long as it is not exhaustively swept out, and doubt in this age is an almost universal impurity. But even when doubt assails, stand by and wait for it to pass, availing yourself if possible of the *satsaṅga* of those who are already advanced on the path, but when that is absent, still holding fast to the principle of the yoga, self-surrender. When distressed within or assailed from without, remember the words of the Gita,

> मच्चित्तः सर्वदुर्गाणि मत्प्रसादात् तरिष्यसि ।

"By giving thyself up in heart and mind to Me, thou shalt cross over all difficulties and perils by My grace," and again,

> सर्वधर्मान् परित्यज्य मामेकं शरणं व्रज ।
> अहं त्वा सर्वपापेभ्यो मोक्षयिष्यामि मा शुचः ।

"Abandon all *dharmas* (all law, rule, means and codes of every kind whether formed by previous habit and belief or imposed from outside) and take refuge in Me alone; I will deliver thee from all sin and evil, — do not grieve." "I will deliver", — you have not to be troubled or struggle yourself as if the responsibility were yours or the result depended on your efforts, a mightier than you is busy with the matter. Neither disease nor calamity nor the rising of sin and impurity in you should cause any alarm. Hold fast only to him. "I will deliver thee from all sin and evil." But the release does not come by a sudden miracle, it comes by a process of purification and these things are a part of the process. They are like the dust that rises in clouds when a room long uncleaned is at last swept out. Though the dust seem to choke you, yet persevere, *mā śucaḥ*.

In order to stand aside, you must know yourself as the Purusha who merely watches, consents to God's work, holds up the Adhar and enjoys the fruits that God gives. The work itself is done by God as Shakti, by Kali, and is offered up by her as a Yajna to Sri Krishna; you are the Yajamana who sees the sacrifice done, whose presence is necessary to every movement of the sacrifice and who tastes its results. This separation of yourself, this renunciation of the *kartṛtva-abhimāna* (the idea of yourself as the doer) is easier if you know what the Adhar is. Above the *buddhi* which is the highest function of mind is the higher *buddhi*, or *vijñāna*, the seat of the *satyadharma*, truth of knowledge, truth of *bhāva*, truth of action, and above this ideal faculty is the *ānanda* or cosmic bliss in which the divine part of you dwells. It is of this *vijñāna* and this *ānanda* that Christ spoke as the kingdom of God that is within you. We at present are awake, *jāgrat*, in the lower movements but *suṣupta*, fast asleep, in the *vijñāna* and *ānanda*; we have to awaken these levels of consciousness within us and their awakening and unmixed activity is the *siddhi* of the yoga. For when that happens, we gain the condition of being which is called in the Gita dwelling in God, of which Sri Krishna speaks when he says, *mayi nivasiṣyasyeva*, "Verily thou shalt dwell in Me." Once it is gained, we are free and blessed and have everything towards which we strive.

The third process of the yoga is to perceive all things as God. First, as a rule, in the process of knowledge one comes to see pervading all space and time one divine impersonal Existence, Sad Atman, without movement, distinction or feature, *śāntam alakṣaṇam*, in which all names and forms seem to stand with a very doubtful or a very minor reality. In this realisation the One may seem to be the only reality and everything else Maya, a purposeless and inexplicable illusion. But afterwards, if you do not stop short and limit yourself by the impersonal realisation, you will come to see the same Atman not only containing and supporting all created things, but informing and filling them, and eventually you will be able to understand that even the names and forms are Brahman. You will then be able to live more and more in the knowledge which the Upanishads and the Gita hold up as the rule of life; you will see the Self in all existing things and all existing things in the Self, *ātmānaṁ sarvabhūteṣu sarvabhūtāni cātmani*; you will be aware of all things as Brahman, *sarvaṁ khalvidaṁ brahma*. But the crowning realisation of this yoga is when you become aware of the whole world as the expression, play or Lila of an infinite divine personality, when you see in all, not the impersonal Sad Atman which is the basis of manifest existence, — although you do not lose that knowledge, — but Sri Krishna who at once is, bases and transcends all manifest and unmanifest existence, *avyakto 'vyaktāt paraḥ*. For behind the Sad Atman is the silence of the Asat which the Buddhist Nihilists realised as the *śūnyam* and beyond that silence is the Paratpara Purusha (*puruṣo vareṇya ādityavarṇas tamasaḥ parastāt*). It is he who has made this world out of his being and is immanent in and sustains it as the infinite-finite Ishwara, *ananta* and *sānta*, Shiva and Narayana, Sri Krishna the Lilamaya who draws all of us to him by his love, compels all of us by his masteries and plays his eternal play of joy and strength and beauty in the manifold world.

The world is only a play of his being, knowledge and delight, *sat*, *cit* and *ānanda*. Matter itself, you will one day realise, is not material, it is not substance but form of consciousness, *guṇa*, the result of quality of being perceived by sense-knowledge. Solidity itself is only a combination of the *guṇas*, *saṁhati* and *dhṛti*, cohesion and permanence, a state of conscious being, nothing else. Matter, life, mind and what is beyond mind, it is all Sri Krishna the Ananta-guna Brahman playing in the world as the Sachchidananda. When we have this realisation, when we dwell in it securely and permanently, all possibilities of grief and sin, fear, delusion, internal strife and pain are driven puissantly from our being. We realise in our experience the truth of the Upanishads,

आनन्दं ब्रह्मणो विद्वान् न बिभेति कुतश्चन ।

"He who possesses the delight of the Brahman has no fear from anything in the world," and that other in the Isha Upanishad,

यस्मिन् सर्वाणि भूतानि आत्मैवाभूद् विजानतः ।
तत्र को मोहः कः शोक एकत्वमनुपश्यतः ॥

"When all created things become one with a man's self by his getting the knowledge (*vijñāna*), thereafter what bewilderment can he have or what grief, when in all things he sees their oneness?" The whole world then appears to us in a changed aspect, as an ocean of beauty, good, light, bliss, exultant movement on a basis of eternal strength and peace. We see all things as *śubha*, *śiva*, *maṅgala*, *ānandamaya*. We become one in soul with all beings, *sarvabhūtātma-bhūtātmā*, and, having steadfastly this experience, are able by contact, by oneness, by the reaching out of love, to communicate it to others, so that we become a centre of the radiation of this divine state, *brāhmī sthiti*, throughout our world.

It is not only in things animate but in things inanimate also that we must see Narayana, experience Shiva, throw our arms around Shakti. When our eyes, that are now blinded by the idea of Matter, open to the supreme Light, we shall find that nothing is inanimate, but all contains, expressed or unexpressed, involved or evolved, secret or manifest or in course of manifestation, not only that state of involved consciousness which we call *annam* or Matter, but also life, mind, knowledge, bliss, divine force and being, — *prāṇa*, *manas*, *vijñāna*, *ānanda*, *cit*, *sat*. In all things the self-conscious personality of God broods and takes the delight of his *guṇas*. Flowers, fruits, earth, trees, metals, all things have a joy in them of which you will become aware, because in all Sri Krishna dwells, *praviśya*, having entered into them, not materially or physically, — because there is no such thing, Space and Time being only conventions and arrangements of perception, the perspective in God's creative Art, — but by *cit*, the divine awareness in his transcendent being.

ईशा वास्यमिदं सर्वं यत् किञ्च जगत्यां जगत् ।

"All this world and every object in this world of Prakriti has been created as a habitation for the Lord."

Nor is it enough to see him in all things and beings, *sarvabhūteṣu*; you must see him in all events, actions, thoughts, feelings, in yourself and others, throughout the world. For this realisation two things are necessary: first, that you should give up to him the fruit of all your actions, secondly, that you should give up to him the actions themselves. Giving up the fruits of action does not mean that you must have the *vairāgya* for the fruits, turn away from them or refuse to act with a given end before you. It means that you must act, not because you want this or that to happen or think it necessary that this or that should happen and your action needed to bring it about, but because it is *kartavyam*, demanded by the Master of your being and must be done with whatever result God is pleased to give. You must put aside what you want and wish to know what God wants; distrust what your heart, your passions or your habitual opinions prefer to hold as right and necessary, and passing beyond them, like Arjuna in the Gita, seek only to know what God has set down as right and necessary. Be strong in the faith that whatever is right and necessary will inevitably happen as the result of your due fulfilment of the *kartavyaṁ karma*, even if it is not the result that you preferred or expected. The power that governs the world is at least as wise as you and it is not absolutely necessary that you should be consulted or indulged in its management; God is seeing to it.

But what is the *kartavyaṁ karma*? It is very difficult to say, — *gahanā karmaṇo gatiḥ*. Most people would translate *kartavyaṁ karma* by the English word and idea, *duty*; if asked to define it, they would say it is the right and moral action, what people understand by right and morality, what you yourself conscientiously think to be right or else what the good of society, the nation or mankind demands of you. But the man who remains bound by these personal or social ideas of duty, necessary as they are for the ignorant to restrain and tame their clamorous desires or their personal egoism, will be indeed what is called a good man, but he will never attain to the fulfilment of this yoga. He will only replace the desire for one kind of fruit by the desire for another kind; he will strive, even more passionately perhaps, for these higher results and be more bitterly grieved by not attaining them. There is no passion so terrible as the passion of the altruist, no egoism so hard to shake as the fixed egoism of virtue, precisely because it is justified in its own eyes and justified in the sight of men and cannot see the necessity for yielding to a higher law. Even if there is no grieving over the results, there will be the labour and strife of the rajasic *kartā*, struggling and fighting, getting eager and getting exhausted, not *triguṇātīta*, always under bondage to the *guṇas*.

It was under the domination of these ideas of personal virtue and social duty that Arjuna refused to fight. Against his reasonings Sri Krishna sets two different ideas, one inferior for the use of the man bound but seeking liberation, another superior for the liberated man, the Shastra and surrender not only of the fruits of the work but of the work itself to God. The virtue of the Shastra is that it sets up a standard outside ourselves, different from our personal desires, reasonings, passions and prejudices, outside our selfishness and self-will, by living up to which in the right spirit we can not only acquire self-control but by reducing even the sattwic *ahaṅkāra* to a minimum prepare ourselves for liberation. In the old days the Shastra was the Vedic Dharma based upon a profound knowledge of man's psychology and the laws of the world, revealing man to himself and showing him how to live according to his nature; afterwards it was the law of the Smritis which tried to do the same thing more roughly by classifying men according to the general classes of which the Vedas speak, the *cāturvarṇya*; today it is little more than blind mechanical custom and habitual social observance, a thing not sattwic but tamasic, not a preparatory discipline for liberation, but a mere bondage.

Even the highest Shastra can be misused for the purposes of egoism, the egoism of virtue and the egoism of prejudice and personal opinion. At its best it is a great means towards the preparation of liberation. It is *śabdabrahma*. But we must not be satisfied with mere preparation, we must, as soon as our eyes are opened, hasten on to actual freedom. The liberated soul and the sadhak of liberation who has surrendered even his actions to God, gets beyond the highest Shastra, *śabdabrahmātivartate*.

The best foundation for the surrender of action is the realisation that Prakriti is doing all our actions at God's command and God through our *svabhāva* determines the action. From that moment the action belongs to him, it is not yours nor the responsibility yours; there is indeed no responsibility, no bondage of Karma, for God has no responsibility, but is in every way master and free. Our actions become not only like the Shastric man's *svabhāvaniyata*, regulated by nature and therefore *dharma*, but the *svabhāva* itself is controlled like a machine by

God. It is not easy for us, full as we are of the Sanskaras of ignorance, to arrive at this stage of knowledge, but there are three stages by which it can be rapidly done. The first is to live in the spirit of the *śloka*, —

त्वया हृषीकेश हृदि स्थितेन यथा नियुक्तोऽस्मि तथा करोमि ।

"According as I am appointed by Thee, O Hrishikesha! seated in my heart, so I act." When this has entered into your daily life, it will be easier to accomplish the second stage and live in the knowledge of the Gita,

ईश्वरः सर्वभूतानां हृद्देशेऽर्जुन तिष्ठति ।
भ्रामयन् सर्वभूतानि यन्त्ररूढानि मायया ॥

"God stands in the heart of all beings, whirling round all, as on a wheel, by the Maya of the three *guṇas*." You will then be able to perceive the action of the three *guṇas* in you and watch the machinery at its work, no longer saying, *tathā karomi*, I do, but *guṇā vartanta eva*, it is merely the *guṇas* that work. One great difficulty in these stages, especially before you can distinguish the action of the *guṇas*, is the perception of the impurity of the *svabhāva*, the haunting idea of sin and virtue. You must always remember that, since you have put yourself in God's hands, he will work out the impurities and you have only to be careful, as you cannot be attached either to *pāpa* or *puṇya*, sin or virtue. For he has repeatedly given the *abhaya vacana*, the assurance of safety. "*Pratijānīhi,*" he says in the Gita, "*na me bhaktaḥ praṇaśyati*, he who is devoted to Me cannot perish."

The third stage comes out of the second, by full realisation of God, or of itself by the grace of God. Not only will the Purusha stand apart and be *triguṇātīta*, beyond the three *guṇas*, but the Prakriti, though using the *guṇas*, will be free from their bondage. Sattwa, as we know it, will disappear into pure *prakāśa* and *jyotiḥ*, and the nature will live in a pure, free and infinite self-existing illumination. Tamas, as we know it, will disappear into pure *śama* or *śānti*, and the nature will take its firm stand on an infinite and ineffable rest and peace. Rajas, as we know it, will disappear into pure *tapas*, and the nature will flow in a free and infinite ocean of divine force. On that foundation of calm and in that heaven of light, action will occur as the spontaneous objective expression of God's knowledge, which is one with God's will. This is the condition of infinity, *ānantya*, in which this struggle of bound and limited sattwa, rajas and tamas is replaced by a mighty harmony of free *prakāśa*, *tapas* and *śama*. And even before you reach that condition, on the way to it, you will find that some mighty force not your own, not situated in your body though possessing and occupying it, is thinking for you, feeling for you, acting for you, your very body as well as your mind and heart being moved by that force and not by yourself. You will enjoy that thought, feeling, action, but will neither possess nor be possessed by it, — *karmāṇi pravilīyante*, your actions will disappear without leaving in you mark or trace, as a wave disappears from the surface of the sea, as water falls from the lotus leaf. Your mind, heart, body will not be yours, but God's; you yourself will be only a centre of being, knowledge and bliss through which God works in that Adhar. This is the condition in which one is utterly *taccittaḥ*, given up in all his conscious being to God, in which there is utter fulfilment of the description,

यस्य नाहंकृतो भावो बुद्धिर्यस्य न लिप्यते ।

"One whose state of being is free from egoism and whose understanding receives no stain." This is the surrender of action to which Sri Krishna gives so much importance.

मयि सर्वाणि कर्माणि संन्यस्याध्यात्मचेतसा ।
निराशीर्निर्ममो भूत्वा युध्यस्व विगतज्वरः ॥

"Laying down all actions upon Me, with thy whole conscious being in *adhyātmayoga*, become free from desire and the sense of belongings; fight, let the fever of thy soul pass from thee." For this great and complete liberation it is necessary that you should be *niḥspṛha*, *nirdvandva* and *nirahaṅkāra*, without the longing and reaching after things, free from the *saṁskāra* of the dualities and free from egoism; for these three things are the chief enemies of self-surrender. If you are *nirdvandva*, you can be *niḥspṛha*, but hardly otherwise, for every *dvandva* creates in the mind by the very nature of the mind some form of *rāgadveṣa*, like and dislike, attraction and repulsion, whether they are the lowest dualities that appeal to the mind through the body, hunger and thirst, heat and cold, physical pleasure and pain, or the middle sorts that appeal to it through the feelings and desires, success and failure, victory and defeat, fortune and misfortune, pleasure and displeasure, joy and grief, hate and love, or the highest which appeal to the mind through the discriminating *buddhi*, virtue and sin, reason and unreason, error and truth. These things can only be put under our feet by complete knowledge, the knowledge that sees God in all things and thus comes to understand the relations of things to each other in his great cosmic purpose, by complete Bhakti which accepts all things with joy, — thus abolishing the *dvandvas*, — because they come from the Beloved or by perfect action offering up all works as a sacrifice to God with an entire indifference to these dualities of success, failure, honour, disgrace, etc., which usually pursue all Karma. Such knowledge, such Bhakti, such Karma come inevitably as the eventual result of the *saṅkalpa* of self-surrender and the practice of it.

But it is *ahaṅkāra* that by making the relation and effect of things on ourselves or on things connected with us the standard of life, makes the *dvandvas* a chain for our bondage. *Ahaṅkāra* in its action on our life and sadhana will be seen to be of three kinds, rajasic, tamasic and sattwic. Rajas binds by desire and the craving in the nature for occupation and activity, it is always reaching after action and the fruit of action; it is in order that we may be free from the rajasic *ahaṅkāra* that we have the command, "Do not do works from the desire of fruit," *mā karma-phala-hetur bhūḥ*, and the command to give up our actions to God. Tamas binds by weakness and the craving in the nature for ease and inaction; it is always sinking into idleness, depression, confusion of mind, fear, disappointment, despondency and despair; it is in order that we may get rid of the tamasic *ahaṅkāra* that we are given the command, "Let there be no attachment to inaction," and the instruction to pursue the yoga always, whether we seem to advance or seem to be standing still or seem even to be going back, always with a calm faith and patient and cheerful perseverance, *anirviṇṇacetasā*. Sattwa binds by knowledge and pleasure; it is always attaching itself to some imperfect realisation, to the idea of one's own virtue, the correctness of one's own opinions and principles or at its highest, as in the case of Arjuna, opposing some personal idea of altruism, justice or virtue against the surrender of our will that God demands of us. It is for the escape from the sattwic *ahaṅkāra* that we have to pass beyond the attachment to the duality of virtue and sin, *ubhe sukṛta-duṣkṛte*.

Each of the *guṇas* working on the *ahaṅkāra* has its particular danger for the sadhak who has made the *saṅkalpa* of self-surrender, but has not yet attained to the full accomplishment of the surrender. The danger of the *rajoguṇa* is when the sadhak is assailed by the pride that thinks, "I am a great sadhak, I have advanced so far, I am a great instrument in God's hands," and similar ideas, or when he attaches himself to the work as God's work which must be carried out, putting himself into it and troubling himself about it as if he had more interest in God's work than God himself and could manage it better. Many, while they are acting all the while in the spirit of rajasic *ahaṅkāra*, persuade themselves that God is working through them and they have no part in the action. This is because they are satisfied with the mere intellectual assent to the idea without waiting for the whole system and life to be full of it. A continual remembrance of God in others and renunciation of individual eagerness (*spṛhā*) are needed and a careful watching of our inner activities until God by the full light of self-knowledge, *jñānadīpena bhāsvatā*, dispels all further chance of self-delusion.

The danger of *tamoguṇa* is twofold, first, when the Purusha thinks, identifying himself with the tamas in him, "I am weak, sinful, miserable, ignorant, good-for-nothing, inferior to this man and inferior to that man, *adhama*, what will God do through me?" — as if God were limited by the temporary capacities or incapacities of his instruments and it were not true that he can make the dumb to talk and the lame to cross the hills, *mūkaṁ karoti vācālaṁ paṅguṁ laṅghayate girim*, — and again when the sadhaka tastes the relief, the tremendous relief of a negative *śānti* and, feeling himself delivered from all troubles and in possession of peace, turns away from life and action and becomes attached to the peace and ease of inaction. Remember always that you too are Brahman and the divine Shakti is working in you; reach out always to the realisation of God's omnipotence and his delight in the Lila. He bids Arjuna work *lokasaṅgrahārthāya*, for keeping the world together, for he does not wish the world to sink back into Prakriti, but insists on your acting as he acts,

उत्सीदेयुरिमे लोका न कुर्यां कर्म चेदहम् ।

"These worlds would be overpowered by tamas and sink into Prakriti if I did not do actions." To be attached to inaction is to give up our action not to God but to our tamasic *ahaṅkāra*.

The danger of the *sattvaguṇa* is when the sadhaka becomes attached to any one-sided conclusion of his reason, to some particular *kriyā* or movement of the sadhana, to the joy of any particular *siddhi* of the yoga, perhaps the sense of purity or the possession of some particular power or the Ananda of the contact with God or the sense of freedom and hungers after it, becomes attached to that only and would have nothing else. Remember that the yoga is not for yourself; for these things, though they are part of the *siddhi*, are not the object of the *siddhi*, for you have decided at the beginning to make no claim upon God but take what he gives you freely and, as for the Ananda, the selfless soul will even forego the joy of God's presence, when that is God's will. You must be free even from the highest sattwic *ahaṅkāra*, even from the subtle ignorance of *mumukṣutva*, the desire of liberation, and take all joy and delight without attachment. You will then be the *siddha* or perfect man of the Gita.

These then are the processes of the yoga, (1) the *saṅkalpa* of *ātmasamarpaṇa*, (2) the standing apart from the Adhar by self-knowledge, (3) the vision of God everywhere and in all things and in all happenings, the surrender of the fruits of action and action itself to God, and the freedom thereby from ignorance, from *ahaṅkāra*, from the *dvandvas*, from desire, so that you are *śuddha*, *mukta*, *siddha*, full of Ananda, pure, free, perfect and blissful in your being. But the processes will be worked out, once the *saṅkalpa* is made, by God's Shakti, by a mighty process of Nature. All that is indispensable on your part is the *anumati* and *smṛti*. *Anumati* is consent, you must give a temporary consent to the movements of the yoga, to all that happens inside or outside you as part of the circumstances of the sadhana, not exulting at the good, not fretting at the evil, not struggling in your heart to keep the one or get rid of the other, but always keeping in mind and giving a permanent assent to that which has to be finally effected. The temporary consent is passive submission to the methods and not positive acceptance of the results. The permanent consent is an anticipatory acceptance of the results, a sort of effortless and desireless exercise of will. It is the constant exercise of this desireless will, an intent aspiration and constant remembrance of the path and its goal which are the *dhṛti* and *utsāha* needed, the necessary steadfastness and zeal of the sadhak; *vyākulatā* or excited, passionate eagerness is more intense, but less widely powerful, and it is disturbing and exhausting, giving intense pleasure and pain in the pursuit but not so vast a bliss in the acquisition. The followers of this path must be like the men of the early yugas, *dhīrāḥ*, the great word of praise in the Upanishads. In the remembrance, the *smṛti* or *smaraṇa*, you must be *apramatta*, free from negligence. It is by the loss of the *smṛti* owing to the rush and onset of the *guṇas* that the yogin becomes *bhraṣṭa*, falls from his firm seat, wanders from his path. But you need not be distressed when the *pramāda* comes and the state of fall or clouded condition seems to persist, for there is no fear for you of a permanent fall since God himself has taken entire charge of you and if you stumble, it is because it is best for you to stumble, as a child by frequent stumbling and falling learns to walk. The necessity of *apramattatā* disappears when you can replace the memory of the yoga and its objects by the continual remembrance of God in all things and happenings, the *nitya anusmaraṇa* of the Gita. For those who can make the full surrender from the beginning there is no question; their path is utterly swift and easy.

It is said in the "Sanatsujatiya" that four things are necessary for *siddhi* — *śāstra*, *utsāha*, *guru* and *kāla* — the teaching of the path, zeal in following it, the Guru and time. Your path is that which I am pointing out, the *utsāha* needed is this *anumati* and this *nitya smaraṇa*, the Guru is God himself and for the rest only time is needed. That God himself is the Guru, you will find when knowledge comes to you; you will see how every little circumstance within you and without you has been subtly planned and brought about by infinite wisdom to carry out the natural process of the yoga, how the internal and external movements are arranged and brought together to work on each other, so as to work out the imperfection and work in the perfection. An almighty love and wisdom are at work for your uplifting. Therefore never be troubled by the time that is being taken, even if it seems very long, but when imperfections and obstructions arise, be *apramatta*, *dhīra*, have the *utsāha*, and leave God to do the rest. Time is necessary. It is a tremendous work that is being done in you, the alteration of your whole human nature into a divine nature, the crowding of centuries of evolution into a few years. You ought not to grudge the time. There are other paths that offer more immediate results or at any rate, by offering you some definite *kriyā* you can work at yourself, give your *ahaṅkāra* the satisfaction of feeling that you are doing something, so many more *prāṇāyāmas* today, so much longer a time for the *āsana*, so many more repetitions of the *japa*, so much done, so much definite progress marked. But once you have chosen this path, you must cleave to it. Those are human methods, not the way that the infinite Shakti works, which moves silently, sometimes imperceptibly to its goal, advances here, seems to pause there, then mightily and triumphantly reveals the grandiose thing that it has done. Artificial paths are like canals hewn by the intelligence of man; you travel easily, safely, surely, but from one given place to another. This path is the broad and trackless ocean by which you can travel widely to all parts of the world and are admitted to the freedom of the infinite. All that you need are the ship, the steering-wheel, the compass, the motive-power and a skilful captain. Your ship is the Brahmavidya, faith is your steering-wheel, self-surrender your compass, the motive-power is she who makes, directs and destroys the worlds at God's command and God himself is your captain. But he has his own way of working and his own time for everything. Watch his way and wait for his time. Understand also the importance of accepting the Shastra and submitting to the Guru and do not do like the Europeans who insist on the freedom of the individual intellect to follow its own fancies and preferences which it calls reasonings, even before it is trained to discern or fit to reason. It is much the fashion nowadays to indulge in metaphysical discussions and philosophical subtleties about Maya and Adwaita and put them in the forefront, making them take the place of spiritual experience. Do not follow that fashion or confuse yourself and waste time on the way by questionings which will be amply and luminously answered when the divine knowledge of the *vijñāna* awakes in you. Metaphysical knowledge has its place, but as a handmaid to spiritual experience, showing it the way sometimes but much more dependent on it and living upon its bounty. By itself it is mere *pāṇḍitya*, a dry and barren thing and more often a stumbling-block than a help. Having accepted this path, follow its Shastra without unnecessary doubt and questioning, keeping the mind plastic to the light of the higher knowledge, gripping firmly what is experienced, waiting for light where things are dark to you, taking without pride what help you can from the living guides who have already trod the path, always patient, never hastening to narrow conclusions, but waiting for a more complete experience and a fuller light, relying on the Jagadguru who helps you from within.

It is necessary to say something about the Mayavada and the modern teachings about the Adwaita because they are much in the air at the present moment and, penetrated with ideas from European rationalism and agnosticism for which Shankara would have been astonished to find himself made responsible, perplex many minds. Remember that one-sided philosophies are always a partial statement of truth. The world, as God has made it, is not a rigid exercise in logic but, like a strain of music, an infinite harmony of many diversities, and his own existence, being free and absolute, cannot be logically defined. Just as the best religion is that which admits the truth of all religions, so the best philosophy is that which admits the truth of all philosophies and gives each its right place. Maya is one realisation, an important one which Shankara overstressed because it was most vivid to his own experience. For yourself leave the word for subordinate use and fix rather on the idea of Lila, a deeper and more penetrating word than Maya. Lila includes the idea of Maya and exceeds it; nor has it that association of the vanity of all things, useless to you who have elected to remain and play with Sri Krishna in Mathura and Brindavan.

God is one but he is not bounded by his unity. We see him here as one who is always manifesting as many, not because he cannot help it, but because he so wills, and outside manifestation he is *anirdeśyam*, indefinable, and cannot be described as either one or many. That is what the Upanishads and other sacred books consistently teach; he is *ekamevādvitīyam*, One and there is no other, but also and consequently he is "this man, yonder woman, that blue-winged bird, this scarlet-eyed." He is *śānta*, he is *ananta*; the Jiva is he. "I am the *aśvattha* tree," says Sri Krishna in the Gita, "I am death, I am Agni Vaishwanara, I am the heat that digests food, I am Vyasa, I am Vasudeva, I am Arjuna." All that is the play of his *caitanya* in his infinite being, his manifestations, and therefore all are real. Maya means nothing more than the freedom of Brahman from the circumstances through which he expresses himself. He is in no way limited by that which we see or think about him. That is the Maya from which we must escape, the Maya of ignorance which takes things as separately existent and not God, not *caitanya*, the illimitable for the really limited, the free for the bound. Do you remember the story of Sri Krishna and the Gopis, how Narada found him differently occupied in each house to which he went, present to each Gopi in a different body, yet always the same Sri Krishna? Apart from the devotional meaning of the story, which you know, it is a good image of his World-Lila. He is *sarva*, everyone, each Purusha with his apparently different Prakriti and action is he, and yet at the same time he is the Purushottama who is with Radha, the Para Prakriti, and can withdraw all these into himself when he wills and put them out again when he wills. From one point of view they are one with him, from another one yet different, from yet another always different because they always exist, latent in him or expressed at his pleasure. There is no profit in disputing about these standpoints. Wait until you see God and know yourself and him and then debate and discussion will be unnecessary.

The goal marked out for us is not to speculate about these things, but to experience them. The call upon us is to grow into the image of God, to dwell in him and with him and be a channel of his joy and might and an instrument of his works. Purified from all that is *aśubha*, transfigured in soul by his touch, we have to act in the world as dynamos of that divine electricity and send it thrilling and radiating through mankind, so that wherever one of us stands, hundreds around may become full of his light and force, full of God and full of Ananda. Churches, Orders, theologies, philosophies have failed to save mankind because they have busied themselves with intellectual creeds, dogmas, rites and institutions, with *ācāraśuddhi* and *darśana*, as if these could save mankind, and have neglected the one thing needful, the power and purification of the soul. We must go back to the one thing needful, take up again Christ's gospel of the purity and perfection of mankind, Mahomed's gospel of perfect submission, self-surrender and servitude to God, Chaitanya's gospel of the perfect love and joy of God in man, Ramakrishna's gospel of the unity of all religions and the divinity of God in man, and, gathering all these streams into one mighty river, one purifying and redeeming Ganges, pour it over the death-in-life of a materialistic humanity as Bhagirath led down the Ganges and flooded with it the ashes of his fathers, so that they may be a resurrection of the soul in mankind and the Satyayuga for a while return to the world. Nor is this the whole object of the Lila or the Yoga; the reason for which the Avatars descend is to raise up man again and again, developing in him a higher and ever higher humanity, a greater and yet greater development of divine being, bringing more and more of heaven again and again upon the earth until our toil is done, our work accomplished and Sachchidananda fulfilled in all even here, even in this material universe. Small is his work, even if he succeeds, who labours for his own salvation or the salvation of a few; infinitely great is his, even if he fail or succeed only partially or for a season, who lives only to bring about peace of soul, joy, purity and perfection among all mankind.

APPENDIX

Explanations of Some Words and Phrases

> "Matter itself, you will one day realise, is not material, it is not substance but form of consciousness, *guṇa*, the result of quality of being perceived by sense-knowledge." (p. 9)

There is no need to put "the" before "quality" — in English that would alter the sense. Matter is not regarded in this passage as a quality of being perceived by sense; I don't think that would have any meaning. It is regarded as a result of a certain power and action of consciousness which presents forms of itself to sense perception and it is this quality of sense-perceivedness, so to speak, that gives them the appearance of Matter, i.e. of a certain kind of substantiality inherent in themselves — but in fact they are not self-existent substantial objects but forms of consciousness. The point is that there is no such thing as the self-existent Matter posited by nineteenth-century Science.

> "chitta" and "chetas"

Chitta is ordinarily used for the mental consciousness in general, thought, feeling, etc. taken together with a stress now on one side or another, sometimes on the feelings as in *citta-pramāthī*, sometimes on the thought-mind — that is why I translated it [on p. 6 (*maccittaḥ*)] "heart and mind" in its wider sense. Chetas can be used in the same way, but it has a different shade of sense, properly speaking, and can include also the movements of the soul, covering the whole consciousness even; [on p. 17] I take it in its most general sense. The translation is not meant to be literal but to render the thought in the line in its fullness. *Adhyātmacetasā* practically amounts to what in English we would describe as a spiritual consciousness.

> "throw our arms around" (p. 10)

It is a figure meaning to comprehend in our consciousness with love and Ananda.

> "the nature" (p. 16, lines 9, 11, 13)

Nature here means the parts of Prakriti in the human being: as it is the condition of the Prakriti that changes with shifting of the gunas and it is this condition of the Prakriti that will become illumined by the transformation of *sattva* into *jyotiḥ*.

> *lokasaṅgrahārthāya* (p. 21) — Does this mean present order?

No. It is in a more general sense the maintenance of the world order which may be a developing, not necessarily a stationary one, an order spiritual, moral etc. and not merely a social order.

GLOSSARY

abhaya vacana — word of assurance.
ācāraśuddhi — purification of outer conduct.
adhama — low, degraded.
ādhāra (Adhar) — support, receptacle; the mental-vital-physical system as a vessel of the spiritual consciousness.
adhyātmayoga (Adhyatmayoga) — spiritual yoga.
advaita (Adwaita) — non-duality, monistic Vedanta.
agni-vaiśvānara (Agni Vaishwanara) — Agni (the godhead of fire) as the universal in Man or universal Power.
ahaṅkāra — ego-sense; egoism.
ānanda (Ananda) — bliss, delight, spiritual delight.
ānandamaya — full of delight.
ananta — infinite.
anantaguṇa — possessing infinite qualities.
ānantya — infinity.
anirdeśyam — indefinable.
anirviṇṇacetasā — undepressed in mind and heart.
annam — food, Matter.
anumati — sanction, consent.
apramatta — free from negligence.
apramattatā— the condition of being free from negligence.
āsana — fixed posture, especially the seated posture.
asat (Asat) — Non-being.
aśubha — inauspicious, evil.
aśvattha — peepal tree; the Tree of Life.
ātman (Atman) — Self, Spirit.
ātmānaṁ sarvabhūteṣu sarvabhūtāni cātmani — the Self in all existing things and all existing things in the Self.
ātmasamarpaṇa — self-surrender.
avatāra (Avatar) — descent or Incarnation of God.
avyakto'vyaktāt paraḥ — the unmanifest Supreme beyond the unmanifest [Bh. Gita 8.20].

bhakti (Bhakti) — devotion, love for God.
bhāva — subjective state or feeling; emotion.
bhoga — enjoyment.
bhraṣṭa — fallen from the way of yoga.
brahman (Brahman) — the Eternal, the Infinite, the Supreme Reality.
brahmavidyā — the knowledge of the Brahman.
buddhi — the discerning intelligence and enlightened will.

caitanya — consciousness.
cāturvarṇya — the four orders or classes of society — the Brahmins, men of learning and thought and knowledge; the Kshatriyas, men of power and action; the Vaishyas, men of commerce and productivity; and the Shudras, men of unskilled labour and service.
caturyuga (Chaturyuga) — the Four Ages (yugas).
cit (Chit) — consciousness.
citta (Chitta) — basic consciousness; mind-stuff, the general stuff of mental consciousness.

darśana — a doctrine or a system of philosophy.
dharma — Law, law of being, standard of Truth, rule or law of action.
dhīra — steadfast.
dhīrāḥ — the steadfast ones.
dhṛti — steadfastness, firmness.
dvāpara-yuga (Dwapara) — the Age in which Truth and untruth are equal.

ekamādvitīyam — one without a second.

gahanā karmaṇo gatiḥ — thick and tangled is the way of works.
guṇa — quality, character; one of the three modes of Nature: sattva, rajas, tamas.

guṇā vartanta eva — it is merely the *guṇa*s that work.
guru — spiritual teacher.

haṭhayoga (Hathayoga) — a system of yoga using the body and the vital functionings as its means of perfection and realisation.
hṛṣīkeśa (Hrishikesha) — an epithet of Krishna.

īśvara (Ishwara) — Lord, Master, God.

jagadguru (Jagadguru) — world-teacher.
jāgrat — the waking state, consciousness of the material world.
japa — repetition of a *mantra* or a name of God.
jīva (Jiva) — individual soul.
jñānadīpena bhāsvatā — with the blazing lamp of knowledge.
jyoti — spiritual light, illumination.

kāla (Kala) — time, the time spirit.
kālī (Kali) — the Divine Mother or Shakti, especially in her aspect of Power.
kali-yuga (Kaliyuga) — the last of the four *yuga*s; the Iron Age, the Age of Untruth and Ignorance.
karma (Karma) — action, work; the chain of action and its consequences.
karmāṇi pravilīyante — actions disappear.
kartā — the doer.
kartavyam — that which has to be done.
kartavyam karma — the thing to be done.
kartṛtva abhimāna — the idea of oneself as the doer.
kriyā — specific practice, process, action.

līlā (Lila) — play; creation as the play of God.
līlāmaya (Lilamaya) — the playful one, the divine player.
lokasaṅgrahārthāya — for the holding together of the world and its peoples.

mā karma-phala-hetur bhūḥ — let not the fruits of thy works be thy motive.
manas — mind.
maṅgala — good, auspicious.
mā śucaḥ — do not grieve.
māyā (Maya) — illusion, unreality; the divine power of illusion which veils the Truth and makes the universe appear as if really existing.
māyāvāda (Mayavada) — Illusionism; the doctrine that the world is unreal, an illusion.
mayi nivasiṣyasyeva — verily thou shalt dwell in me.
mokṣa — spiritual liberation.
mūkaṁ karoti vācālaṁ paṅguṁ laṅghayate girim — he makes the dumb to talk and the lame to cross over the hills.
mukta — one who is liberated.
mukti (Mukti) — spiritual liberation.
mumukṣutva — the desire for liberation.

nārāyaṇa (Narayana) — the Divine.
na me bhaktaḥ praṇaśyati — he who is devoted to me cannot perish.
niḥspṛha — free from desire.
nirahaṅkāra — free from egoism.
nirdvandva — free from the dualities.
nitya anusmaraṇa — constant remembrance.
nityamukta — eternally free.
nitya smaraṇa — constant remembrance.

pāṇḍitya — learning, scholarship.
pāpa — sin.
parā prakṛti (Para Prakriti) — higher Nature, supreme Nature.
parātpara puruṣa (Paratpara Purusha) — the Being higher than the highest.
prakāśa — light, divine light; manifestation.

prakṛti (Prakriti) — Nature, Nature-Force; the Lord's executive force.
pramāda — negligence, carelessness; error.
prāṇa — life-energy, vital force; the first of the five *prāṇa*s, the breath.
prāṇāyāma — control of the vital currents in the body by breathing exercises.
pratijānīhi — know thou for certain.
praviśya — having entered.
puṇya — virtue, merit.
pūrṇayoga (Purnayoga) — the integral Yoga.
puruṣa (Purusha) — conscious Being; Person.
puruṣottama (Purushottama) — the Supreme divine Person.
puruṣo vareṇya ādityavarṇas tamasaḥ parastāt — the excellent Purusha, of the colour of the sun, beyond darkness.

rāgadveṣa — like and dislike, attraction and repulsion.
rajas (rajas) — the quality of Nature that energises and drives to action; the mode of action, desire and passion.
rājasika (rajasic) — of the nature of rajas, the quality of action, desire and passion.
rājayoga (Raja Yoga) — a system of yoga primarily using the process of mental concentration as its means of spiritual experience and realisation.
rajoguṇa — the quality of rajas; one of the three *guṇa*s.

śabda-brahma — Brahman as sound; the Word; the Shastra.
śabdabrahmātivartate — passes beyond the *śabdabrahma* (the written word or Shastra).
saccidānanda (Sachchidananda) — Existence-Consciousness-Bliss.
sad-ātman (Sad Atman) — the Self as pure Existence.
sādhaka (sadhak) — one who practises a spiritual discipline.
sādhanā (sadhana) — spiritual practice or discipline.
śakti (Shakti) — force, power; the Divine Power; the Divine Mother.

sama — equal, even.
śama (Shama) — the divine quiet, peace.
saṁhati — close combination, assemblage, massiveness.
saṁskāra (Sanskara) — fundamental tendency, habitual impulsion formed by one's past.
saṁyama — control; in Rajayoga, the concentration or dwelling of the consciousness on a particular object.
saṅkalpa — resolution, will, determination.
sānta — [sa+anta] having an end, finite, limited.
śāntam alakṣaṇam — calm, featureless.
śānti — peace, spiritual calm.
sarva — all.
sarvabhūtātma-bhūtātmā — one whose self has become the self of all existences.
sarvabhūteṣu — in all beings, in all existences.
sarvaṁ khalvidaṁ brahma — verily all this is the *brahman.*
śāstra (Shastra) — scripture; systematised teaching or science.
sat (Sat) — Being, existence; the right, the highest good.
satsaṅga — association with good respectable people.
sattva (sattwa) — the quality of Nature that illumines and clarifies; the mode of light and poise and peace.
sattvaguṇa — the quality of sattwa; one of the three *guṇas.*
satyadharma — the Law of the Truth.
satyayuga (Satyayuga) — the Age of Truth.
siddha (siddha) — the perfected soul, one perfect in the Yoga.
siddhi — yogic perfection.
śiva (Shiva) — good, auspicious; one of the gods of the Hindu trinity, the Lord of tapas, concentration and renunciation.
śloka — verse.
smaraṇa — remembrance, memory.
smṛti (Smriti) — remembrance; traditional or man-made laws.
spṛhā — eagerness.
śubha — good.
śuddha — pure.

śūnyam — nothingness, void.
svabhāva — the nature proper to each being.
svabhāvaniyata — regulated by nature.

taccittaḥ — given up in all his conscious being to That.
tamas (tamas) — the quality of Nature that obscures or darkens; the mode of ignorance and inertia.
tāmasika (tamasic) — of the nature of tamas, the quality of ignorance and inertia.
tamoguṇa — the quality of tamas; one of the three *guṇa*s.
tapas (tapas) — illumined Energy; spiritual Power.
tathā karomi — so I act.
tretā (Treta) — the Treta Yuga, the Age following the Satya Yuga in which three parts belong to Truth and one to untruth.
triguṇātīta — beyond the three *guṇa*s.
trimārga (Trimarga) — the triple path of Yoga; the paths of *jñāna* (knowledge), *bhakti* (devotion) and *karma* (works).

ubhe sukṛtaduṣkṛte — both virtue and sin.
utsāha — zeal; patient and persistent action.

vairāgya — distaste or disgust for the world and life.
vijñāna — the higher knowledge.
vyākulatā — excited passionate eagerness.

yajamāna (Yajamana) — one who performs a *yajña* or sacrifice.
yajña (Yajna) — sacrifice.
yaugika (Yogic) — relating to the Yoga.
yoga (yoga) — union with the Divine; the conscious seeking or the method used for gaining union with the Divine.
yogin (yogin) — one who practises yoga, especially one established in spiritual realisation.
yuga (yuga) — astronomical cycle or Age, said to be four in number, viz. *satya*, *tretā*, *dvāpara* and *kali.*

This collection consists of illuminating extracts from Sri Aurobindo's letters to disciples.

"This Yoga implies not only the realisation of God, but an entire consecration and change of the inner and outer life till it is fit to manifest a divine consciousness and become part of a divine work. This means an inner discipline far more exacting and difficult than mere ethical and physical austerities. One must not enter on this path, far vaster and more arduous than most ways of Yoga, unless one is sure of the psychic call and of one's readiness to go through to the end."

– Sri Aurobindo

ISBN 978-81-7058-057-7
Rs 35

D0379120

LIGHTS ON YOGA

SRI AUROBINDO

LIGHTS ON YOGA

SRI AUROBINDO ASHRAM
PONDICHERRY

First edition 1935
Ninth edition 1981
Eighth impression 2013

Rs 35
ISBN 978-81-7058-057-7

Published by Sri Aurobindo Ashram Publication Department
Pondicherry - 605 002
Web http://www.sabda.in

Printed at Sri Aurobindo Ashram Press, Pondicherry
PRINTED IN INDIA

PUBLISHER'S NOTE

This booklet was first published in 1935 with the following note:

> These are extracts from letters written by Sri Aurobindo to his disciples in answer to their queries. They have been put together and arranged so as to be of help to some aspirants for the understanding and practice of the Yoga.

The extracts were compiled by Sri Aurobindo's secretary. Sri Aurobindo approved the arrangement and lightly revised the texts.

It has recently been found that the notes on purity, faithfulness and sincerity on pages 23 and 24 were written by the Mother. They remain here in their original places in the compilation.

CONTENTS

THE GOAL

The way of Yoga followed here has a different purpose from others, – for its aim is not only to rise out of the ordinary ignorant world-consciousness into the divine consciousness, but to bring the supramental power of that divine consciousness down into the ignorance of mind, life and body, to transform them, to manifest the Divine here and create a divine life in Matter. This is an exceedingly difficult aim and difficult Yoga; to many or most it will seem impossible. All the established forces of the ordinary ignorant world-consciousness are opposed to it and deny it and try to prevent it, and the Sadhak will find his own mind, life and body full of the most obstinate impediments to its realisation. If you can accept the ideal whole-heartedly, face all the difficulties, leave the past and its ties behind you and are ready to give up everything and risk everything for this divine possibility, then only can you hope to discover by experience the Truth behind it.

The Sadhana of this Yoga does not proceed through any set mental teaching or prescribed forms of meditation, *mantras* or others, but by aspiration, by a self-concentration inwards or upwards, by self-opening to an Influence, to the Divine Power above us and its workings, to the Divine Presence in the heart and by the rejection of all that is foreign to these things. It is only by faith, aspiration and surrender that this self-opening can come.

*

The only creation for which there is any place here is the supramental, the bringing of the divine Truth down on the earth, not only into the mind and vital but into the body and into Matter. Our object is not to remove all "limitations" on the expansion of the ego or to give a free field and make unlimited room for the fulfilment of the ideas of the human mind or the desires of the ego-centred life-force. None of us are here to "do as we like", or to create a world in which we shall at last be able to do as we like; we are here to do what the Divine wills and to create a world in which the Divine Will can manifest its truth no longer deformed by human ignorance or perverted and mistranslated by vital desire. The work which the Sadhak of the supramental Yoga has to do is not his own work for which he can lay down his own conditions, but the work of the Divine which he has to do according to the conditions laid down by the Divine. Our Yoga is not for our own sake but for the sake of the Divine. It is not our own personal manifestation that we are to seek, the manifestation of the individual ego freed from all bounds and from all bonds, but the manifestation of the Divine. Of that manifestation our own spiritual liberation, perfection, fullness is to be a result and a part, but not in any egoistic sense or for any ego-centred or self-seeking purpose. This liberation, perfection, fullness too must not be pursued for our own sake, but for the sake of the Divine.

*

This Yoga implies not only the realisation of God,

but an entire consecration and change of the inner and outer life till it is fit to manifest a divine consciousness and become part of a divine work. This means an inner discipline far more exacting and difficult than mere ethical and physical austerities. One must not enter on this path, far vaster and more arduous than most ways of Yoga, unless one is sure of the psychic call and of one's readiness to go through to the end.

*

In the former Yogas it was the experience of the Spirit which is always free and one with the Divine that was sought. The nature had to change only enough to prevent its being an obstacle to that knowledge and experience. The complete change down to the physical was only sought for by a few and then more as a "siddhi" than anything else, not as the manifestation of a new Nature in the earth-consciousness.

*

All the consciousness in the human being who is the mental embodied in living Matter has to rise so as to meet the higher consciousness; the higher consciousness has also to descend into mind, into life, into Matter. In that way the barriers will be removed and the higher consciousness will be able to take up the whole lower naturc and transform it by the power of the supermind.

The earth is a material field of evolution. Mind and Life, Supermind, Sachchidananda are in principle involved there in the earth-consciousness; but only Matter is at

first organised; then life descends from the life plane and gives shape and organisation and activity to the life principle in Matter, creates the plant and animal; then mind descends from the mind plane, creating man. Now Supermind is to descend so as to create a supramental race.

*

In order to get the dynamic realisation it is not enough to rescue the Purusha from subjection to Prakriti; one must transfer the allegiance of the Purusha from the lower Prakriti with its play of ignorant Forces to the Supreme Divine Shakti, the Mother.

It is a mistake to identify the Mother with the lower Prakriti and its mechanism of forces. Prakriti here is a mechanism only which has been put forth for the working of the evolutionary ignorance. As the ignorant mental, vital or physical being is not itself the Divine, although it comes from the Divine – so the mechanism of Prakriti is not the Divine Mother. No doubt something of her is there in and behind this mechanism maintaining it for the evolutionary purpose; but what she is in herself is not a Shakti of Avidya, but the Divine Consciousness, Power, Light, Para Prakriti to whom we turn for the release and the divine fulfilment.

The realisation of the Purusha consciousness calm, free, observing the play of forces but not attached or involved in them is a means of liberation. The calm, the detachment, a peaceful strength and joy *(ātmarati)* must be brought down into the vital and physical as well as into the mind. If this is established, one is no longer a

prey to the turmoil of the vital forces. But this calm, peace, silent strength and joy is only the first descent of the Power of the Mother into the Adhar. Beyond that is a Knowledge, an executive Power, a dynamic Ananda which is not that of the ordinary Prakriti even at its best and most Sattwic, but Divine in its nature.

First, however, the calm, the peace, the liberation is needed. To try to bring down the dynamic side too soon is not advisable, for then it would be a descent into a troubled and impure nature unable to assimilate it and serious perturbations might be the consequence.

*

If the Supermind were not to give us a greater and completer truth than any of the lower planes, it would not be worth while trying to reach it. Each plane has its own truths. Some of them are no longer true on a higher plane; e.g., desire and ego were truths of the mental, vital and physical Ignorance – a man there without ego or desire would be a Tamasic automaton. As we rise higher, ego and desire appear no longer as truths, they are falsehoods disfiguring the true person and the true will. The struggle between the Powers of Light and the Powers of Darkness is a truth here – as we ascend above, it becomes less and less of a truth and in the supermind it has no truth at all. Other truths remain but change their character, importance, place in the whole. The difference or contrast between the Personal and Impersonal is a truth of the Overmind – there is no separate truth of them in the Supermind, they are inseparably one. But

one who has not mastered and lived the truths of Overmind cannot reach the supramental Truth. The incompetent pride of man's mind makes a sharp distinction and wants to call all else untruth and leap at once to the highest truth whatever it may be – but that is an ambitious and arrogant error. One has to climb the stairs and rest one's feet firmly on each step in order to reach the summit.

*

It is a mistake to dwell too much on the lower nature and its obstacles, which is the negative side of the Sadhana. They have to be seen and purified, but preoccupation with them as the one important thing is not helpful. The positive side of experience of the descent is the more important thing. If one waits for the lower nature to be purified entirely and for all time before calling down the positive experience, one might have to wait for ever. It is true that the more the lower nature is purified, the easier is the descent of the higher Nature, but it is also and more true that the more the higher Nature descends, the more the lower is purified. Neither the complete purification nor the permanent and perfect manifestation can come all at once, it is a matter of time and patient progress. The two (purification and manifestation) go on progressing side by side and become more and more strong to play into each other's hands – that is the usual course of the Sadhana.

*

Intensities like that do not remain so long as the consciousness is not transformed – there has to be a period of assimilation. When the being is unconscious, the assimilation goes on behind the veil or below the surface and meanwhile the surface consciousness sees only dullness and loss of what it had got; but when one is conscious, then one can see the assimilation going on and one sees that nothing is lost, it is only a quiet settling in of what has come down.

The vastness, the overwhelming calm and silence in which you feel merged is what is called the Atman or the silent Brahman. It is the whole aim of many Yogas to get this realisation of Atman or silent Brahman and live in it. In our Yoga it is only the first stage of the realisation of the Divine and of that growing of the being into the higher or divine Consciousness which we call transformation.

*

The true being may be realised in one or both of two aspects – the Self or Atman and the soul or Antaratman, psychic being, Chaitya Purusha. The difference is that one is felt as universal, the other as individual supporting the mind, life and body. When one first realises the Atman one feels it separate from all things, existing in itself and detached, and it is to this realisation that the image of the dry coconut fruit may apply. When one realises the psychic being, it is not like that; for this brings the sense of union with the Divine and dependence upon It and sole consecration to the Divine alone and the power

to change the nature and discover the true mental, the true vital, the true physical being in oneself. Both realisations are necessary for this Yoga.

The "I" or the little ego is constituted by Nature and is at once a mental, vital and physical formation meant to aid in centralising and individualising the outer consciousness and action. When the true being is discovered, the utility of the ego is over and this formation has to disappear – the true being is felt in its place.

*

The three Gunas become purified and refined and changed into their divine equivalents: *sattva* becomes *jyoti,* the authentic spiritual light; *rajas* becomes *tapas,* the tranquilly intense divine force; *tamas* becomes *śama,* the divine quiet, rest, peace.

*

There are three powers of the cosmos to which all things are subject – creation, preservation and destruction; whatever is created lasts for a time, then begins to crumble down. The taking away of the Force of destruction implies a creation that will not be destroyed but last and develop always. In the Ignorance destruction is necessary for progress – in the Knowledge, the Truth-creation, the law is that of a constant unfolding without any Pralaya.

PLANES AND PARTS OF THE BEING

Men do not know themselves and have not learned to distinguish the different parts of their being; for these are usually lumped together by them as mind, because it is through a mentalised perception and understanding that they know or feel them; therefore they do not understand their own states and actions, or, if at all, then only on the surface. It is part of the foundation of Yoga to become conscious of the great complexity of our nature, see the different forces that move it and get over it a control of directing knowledge. We are composed of many parts each of which contributes something to the total movement of our consciousness, our thought, will, sensation, feeling, action, but we do not see the origination or the course of these impulsions; we are aware only of their confused and pell-mell results on the surface upon which we can at best impose nothing better than a precarious shifting order.

The remedy can only come from the parts of the being that are already turned towards the Light. To call in the light of the Divine Consciousness from above, to bring the psychic being to the front and kindle a flame of aspiration which will awaken spiritually the outer mind and set on fire the vital being, is the way out.

*

Yoga means union with the Divine – a union either transcendental (above the universe) or cosmic (univer-

sal) or individual or, as in our Yoga, all three together. Or it means getting into a consciousness in which one is no longer limited by the small ego, personal mind, personal vital and body but is in union with the supreme Self or with the universal (cosmic) consciousness or with some deeper consciousness within in which one is aware of one's own soul, one's own inner being and of the real truth of existence. In the Yogic consciousness one is not only aware of things, but of forces, not only of forces, but of the conscious being behind the forces. One is aware of all this not only in oneself but in the universe.

There is a force which accompanies the growth of the new consciousness and at once grows with it and helps it to come about and to perfect itself. This force is the Yoga-Shakti. It is here coiled up and asleep in all the centres of our inner being (Chakras) and is at the base what is called in the Tantras the Kundalini Shakti. But it is also above us, above our head as the Divine Force – not there coiled up, involved, asleep, but awake, scient, potent, extended and wide; it is there waiting for manifestation and to this Force we have to open ourselves – to the power of the Mother. In the mind it manifests itself as a divine mind-force or a universal mind-force and it can do everything that the personal mind cannot do; it is then the Yogic mind-force. When it manifests and acts in the vital or the physical in the same way, it is there apparent as a Yogic life-force or a Yogic body-force. It can awake in all these forms, bursting outwards and upwards, extending itself into wideness from below; or it can descend and become there a definite power for

things; it can pour downwards into the body, working, establishing its reign, extending into wideness from above, link the lowest in us with the highest above us, release the individual into a cosmic universality or into absoluteness and transcendence.

*

In the process of our Yoga the centres have each a fixed psychological use and general function which base all their special powers and functionings. The *mūlādhāra* governs the physical down to the subconscient; the abdominal centre – *svādhiṣṭhāna* – governs the lower vital; the navel centre – *nābhipadma* or *maṇipura* – governs the larger vital; the heart centre – *hṛdpadma* or *anāhata* – governs the emotional being; the throat centre – *viśuddha* – governs the expressive and externalising mind; the centre between the eye-brows – *ājñācakra* – governs the dynamic mind, will, vision, mental formation; the thousand-petalled lotus – *sahasradala* – above commands the higher thinking mind, houses the still higher illumined mind and at the highest opens to the intuition through which or else by an overflooding directness the overmind can have with the rest communication or an immediate contact.

*

In our Yoga we mean by the subconscient that quite submerged part of our being in which there is no wakingly conscious and coherent thought, will or feeling or organised reaction, but which yet receives obscurely the impressions of all things and stores them up in itself and

from it too all sorts of stimuli, or persistent habitual movements, crudely repeated or disguised in strange forms can surge up into dream or into the waking nature. For if these impressions rise up most in dream in an incoherent and disorganised manner, they can also and do rise up into our waking consciousness as a mechanical repetition of old thoughts, old mental, vital and physical habits or an obscure stimulus to sensations, actions, emotions which do not originate in or from our conscious thought or will and are even often opposed to its perceptions, choice or dictates. In the subconscient there is an obscure mind full of obstinate Sanskaras, impressions, associations, fixed notions, habitual reactions formed by our past, an obscure vital full of the seeds of habitual desires, sensations and nervous reactions, a most obscure material which governs much that has to do with the condition of the body. It is largely responsible for our illnesses; chronic or repeated illnesses are indeed mainly due to the subconscient and its obstinate memory and habit of repetition of whatever has impressed itself upon the body-consciousness. But this subconscient must be clearly distinguished from the subliminal parts of our being such as the inner or subtle physical consciousness, the inner vital or inner mental; for these are not at all obscure or incoherent or ill-organised, but only veiled from our surface consciousness. Our surface constantly receives something, inner touches, communications or influences, from these sources but does not know for the most part whence they come.

*

There is a vital plane (self-existent) above the material universe which we see; there is a mental plane (self-existent) above the vital and material. These three together, – mental, vital, physical, – are called the triple universe of the lower hemisphere. They have been established in the earth-consciousness by evolution – but they exist in themselves before the evolution, above the earth-consciousness and the material plane to which the earth belongs.

*

There is behind all the vital nature in man his true vital being concealed and immobile which is quite different from the surface vital nature. The surface vital is narrow, ignorant, limited, full of obscure desires, passions, cravings, revolts, pleasures and pains, transient joys and griefs, exultations and depressions. The true vital being, on the contrary, is wide, vast, calm, strong, without limitations, firm and immovable, capable of all power, all knowledge, all Ananda. It is moreover without ego, for it knows itself to be a projection and instrument of the Divine: it is the divine Warrior, pure and perfect; in it is an instrumental Force for all divine realisations. It is the true vital being that has become awake and come in front within you. In the same way there is too a true mental being, a true physical being. When these are manifest, then you are aware of a double existence in you: that behind is always calm and strong, that on the surface alone is troubled and obscure. But if the true being behind remains stable and you live in it,

then the trouble and obscurity remain only on the surface; in this condition the exterior parts can be dealt with more potently and they are also made free and perfect.

*

The "Mind" in the ordinary use of the word covers indiscriminately the whole consciousness, for man is a mental being and mentalises everything; but in the language of this Yoga the words "mind" and "mental" are used to connote specially the part of the nature which has to do with cognition and intelligence, with ideas, with mental or thought perceptions, the reactions of thought to things, with the truly mental movements and formations, mental vision and will, etc., that are part of his intelligence. The vital has to be carefully distinguished from mind, even though it has a mind element transfused into it; the vital is the Life-nature made up of desires, sensations, feelings, passions, energies of action, will of desire, reactions of the desire-soul in man and of all that play of possessive and other related instincts, anger, fear, greed, lust, etc., that belong to this field of the nature. Mind and vital are mixed up on the surface of the consciousness, but they are quite separate forces in themselves and as soon as one gets behind the ordinary surface consciousness one sees them as separate, discovers their distinction and can with the aid of this knowledge analyse their surface mixtures. It is quite possible and even usual during a time shorter or longer, sometimes very long, for the mind to accept the Divine or the Yogic

ideal while the vital is unconvinced and unsurrendered and goes obstinately on its way of desire, passion and attraction to the ordinary life. Their division or their conflict is the cause of most of the more acute difficulties of the Sadhana.

*

The mental being within watches, observes and passes judgment on all that happens in you. The psychic does not watch and observe in this way like a witness, but it feels and knows spontaneously in a much more direct and luminous way, by the very purity of its own nature and the divine instinct within it, and so, whenever it comes to the front it reveals at once what are the right and what the wrong movements in your nature.

The being of man is composed of these elements – the psychic behind supporting all, the inner mental, vital and physical, and the outer, quite external nature of mind, life and body which is their instrument of expression. But above all is the central being (Jivatman) which uses them all for its manifestation: it is a portion of the Divine Self; but this reality of himself is hidden from the external man who replaces this inmost self and soul of him by the mental and vital ego. It is only those who have begun to know themselves that become aware of their true central being; but still it is always there standing behind the action of mind, life and body and is most directly represented by the psychic which is itself a spark of the Divine. It is by the growth of the psychic element in one's nature that one begins to come into conscious

touch with one's central being above. When that happens and the central being uses a conscious will to control and organise the movements of the nature, it is then that one has a real, a spiritual as opposed to a partial and merely mental or moral self-mastery.

*

The phrase "central being" in our Yoga is usually applied to the portion of the Divine in us which supports all the rest and survives through death and birth. This central being has two forms – above, it is Jivatman, our true being, of which we become aware when the higher self-knowledge comes, – below, it is the psychic being which stands behind mind, body and life. The Jivatman is above the manifestation in life and presides over it; the psychic being stands behind the manifestation in life and supports it.

The natural attitude of the psychic being is to feel itself as the Child, the Son of God, the Bhakta; it is a portion of the Divine, one in essence, but in the dynamics of the manifestation there is always even in identity a difference. The Jivatman, on the contrary, lives in the essence and can merge itself in identity with the Divine; but it too, the moment it presides over the dynamics of the manifestation, knows itself as one centre of the multiple Divine, not as the Parameshwara. It is important to remember the distinction; for, otherwise, if there is the least vital egoism, one may begin to think of oneself as an Avatar or lose balance like Hridaya with Ramakrishna.

*

The Spirit is the Atman, Brahman, Essential Divine.

When the One Divine manifests its ever inherent multiplicity, this essential Self or Atman becomes for that manifestation the central being who presides from above over the evolution of its personalities and terrestrial lives here, but is itself an eternal portion of the Divine and prior to the terrestrial manifestation – *parā prakṛtir jīvabhūtā.*

In this lower manifestation, *aparā prakṛti,* this eternal portion of the Divine appears as the soul, a spark of the Divine Fire, supporting the individual evolution, supporting the mental, vital and physical being. The psychic being is the spark growing into a Fire, evolving with the growth of the consciousness. The psychic being is therefore evolutionary, not like the Jivatman prior to the evolution.

But man is not aware of the self or Jivatman, he is aware only of his ego, or he is aware of the mental being which controls the life and the body. But more deeply he becomes aware of his soul or psychic being as his true centre, the Purusha in the heart; the psychic is the central being in the evolution, it proceeds from and represents the Jivatman, the eternal portion of the Divine. When there is the full consciousness, the Jivatman and the psychic being join together.

The ego is a formation of Nature; but it is not a formation of physical nature alone, therefore it does not cease with the body. There is a mental and vital ego also.

The base of the material consciousness here is not only the Ignorance, but the Inconscience – that is, the

consciousness is involved in form of Matter and energy of Matter. It is not only the material consciousness but the vital and the mental too that are separated from the Truth by the Ignorance.

*

The word Jiva has two meanings in the Sanskritic tongues – "living creatures"* and the spirit individualised and upholding the living being in its evolution from birth to birth. In the latter sense the full term is Jivatman – the Atman, spirit or eternal self of the living being. It is spoken of figuratively by the Gita as "an eternal portion of the Divine" – but the word fragmentation (used by you) is too strong, it could be applicable to the forms, but not to the spirit in them. Moreover, the multiple Divine is an eternal reality antecedent to the creation here. An elaborate description of the Jivatman would be: "the multiple Divine manifested here as the individualised self or spirit of the created being." The Jivatman in its essence does not change or evolve, its essence stands above the personal evolution; within the evolution itself it is represented by the evolving psychic being which supports all the rest of the nature.

The Adwaita Vedanta (Monism) declares that the Jiva has no real existence, as the Divine is indivisible. Another school attributes a real but not an independent existence to the Jiva – it is, they say, one in essence, different in manifestation, and as the manifestation is real,

* In Bengal when one is about to kill a small animal, people often protest saying "Don't kill – it is Krishna's Jiva (His living creature)."

eternal and not an illusion, it cannot be called unreal. The dualistic schools affirm the Jiva as an independent category or stand on the triplicity of God, Soul and Nature.

*

The soul takes birth each time, and each time a mind, life and body are formed out of the materials of universal Nature according to the soul's past evolution and its need for the future.

When the body is dissolved, the vital goes into the vital plane and remains there for a time, but after a time the vital sheath disappears. The last to dissolve is the mental sheath. Finally, the soul or psychic being retires into the psychic world to rest there till a new birth is close.

This is the general course for ordinarily developed human beings. There are variations according to the nature of the individual and his development. For example, if the mental is strongly developed, then the mental being can remain; so also can the vital, provided they are organised by and centred around the true psychic being; they share the immortality of the psychic.

The soul gathers the essential elements of its experiences in life and makes that its basis of growth in the evolution; when it returns to birth it takes up with its mental, vital, physical sheaths so much of its Karma as is useful to it in the new life for further experience.

It is really for the vital part of the being that Shraddha and rites are done – to help the being to get rid of the

vital vibrations which still attach it to the earth or to the vital worlds, so that it may pass quickly to its rest in the psychic peace.

*

The consciousness in the individual widens itself into the cosmic consciousness outside and can have any kind of dealing with it, penetrate, know its movements, act upon it or receive from it, even become commensurate with or contain it, which is what was meant in the language of the old Yogas by having the Brahmanda within you.

The cosmic consciousness is that of the universe, of the cosmic spirit and cosmic Nature with all the beings and forces within it. All that is as much conscious as a whole as the individual separately is, though in a different way. The consciousness of the individual is part of this, but a part feeling itself as a separate being. Yet all the time most of what he is comes into him from the cosmic consciousness. But there is a wall of separative ignorance between. Once it breaks down he becomes aware of the cosmic Self, of the consciousness of the cosmic Nature, of the forces playing in it, etc. He feels all that as he now feels physical things and impacts. He finds it all to be one with his larger or universal self.

There is the universal mental, the universal vital, the universal physical Nature and it is out of a selection of their forces and movements that the individual mind, vital and physical are made. The soul comes from beyond this nature of mind, life and body. It belongs to the transcendent and because of it we can open to the

higher Nature beyond.

The Divine is always One that is Many. The individual spirit is part of the "Many" side of the One, and the psychic being is what it puts forth to evolve here in the earth-nature. In liberation the individual self realises itself as the One (that is yet Many). It may plunge into the One and merge or hide itself in its bosom – that is the *laya* of the Adwaita; it may feel its oneness and yet as part of the Many that is One enjoy the Divine, that is the Dwaitadwaita liberation; it may lay stress on its Many aspect and be possessed by the Divine, the Vishistadwaita, or go on playing with Krishna in the eternal Vrindavan, the Dwaita liberation. Or it may, even being liberated, remain in the Lila or manifestation or descend into it as often as it likes. The Divine is not bound by human philosophies – it is free in its play and free in its essence.

*

What is meant by Prakriti or Nature is the outer or executive side of the Shakti or Conscious Force which forms and moves the worlds. This outer side appears here to be mechanical, a play of the forces, Gunas, etc. Behind it is the living consciousness and Force of the Divine, the divine Shakti. The Prakriti itself is divided into the lower and higher, – the lower is the Prakriti of the Ignorance, the Prakriti of mind, life and Matter separated in consciousness from the Divine; the higher is the Divine Prakriti of Sachchidananda with its manifesting power of Supermind, always aware of the Divine and free from Ignorance and its consequences. Man so long as he is in

the ignorance is subject to the lower Prakriti, but by spiritual evolution he becomes aware of the higher Nature and seeks to come into contact with it. He can ascend into it and it can descend into him – such an ascent and descent can transform the lower nature of mind, life and Matter.

*

The Overmind has to be reached and brought down before the supermind descent is at all possible – for the Overmind is the passage through which one passes from Mind to Supermind.

It is from the Overmind that all these different arrangements of the creative Truth of things originate. Out of the Overmind they come down to the Intuition and are transmitted from it to the Illumined and Higher Mind to be arranged there for our intelligence. But they lose more and more of their power and certitude in the transmission as they come down to the lower levels. What energy of directly perceived Truth they have is lost in the human mind; for to the human intellect they present themselves only as speculative ideas, not as realised Truth, not as direct sight, a dynamic vision coupled with a concrete undeniable experience.

*

Supermind is between the Sachchidananda and the lower creation. It alone contains the self-determining Truth of the Divine Consciousness and is necessary for a Truth-creation.

One can of course realise Sachchidananda in relation to the mind, life and body also – but then it is something stable, supporting by its presence the lower Prakriti, but not transforming it. The Supermind alone can transform the lower nature.

*

Sachchidananda is the One with a triple aspect. In the Supreme the three are not three but one – existence is consciousness, consciousness is bliss, and they are thus inseparable, not only inseparable but so much each other that they are not distinct at all. In the superior planes of manifestation they become triune – although inseparable, one can be made more prominent and base or lead the others. In the lower planes below they become separable in appearance, though not in their secret reality, and one can exist phenomenally without the others so that we become aware of what seems to us an inconscient or a painful existence or a consciousness without Ananda. Indeed, without this separation of them in experience pain and ignorance and falsehood and death and what we call inconscience could not have manifested themselves – there could not have been this evolution of a limited and suffering consciousness out of the universal nescience of Matter.

SURRENDER AND OPENING

The whole principle of this Yoga is to give oneself entirely to the Divine alone and to nobody and nothing else, and to bring down into ourselves by union with the Divine Mother all the transcendent light, power, wideness, peace, purity, Truth-consciousness and Ananda of the Supramental Divine.

*

Radha is the personification of the absolute love for the Divine, total and integral in all parts of the being from the highest spiritual to the physical, bringing the absolute self-giving and total consecration of all the being and calling down into the body and the most material nature the supreme Ananda.

*

Purity is to accept no other influence but only the influence of the Divine.

*

Faithfulness is to admit and to manifest no other movements but only the movements prompted and guided by the Divine.

*

Sincerity means to lift all the movements of the being to the level of the highest consciousness and realisation

already attained.

Sincerity exacts the unification and harmonisation of the whole being in all its parts and movements around the central Divine Will.

*

The Divine gives itself to those who give themselves without reserve and in all their parts to the Divine. For them the calm, the light, the power, the bliss, the freedom, the wideness, the heights of knowledge, the seas of Ananda.

*

Talk of surrender or a mere idea or tepid wish for integral consecration will not do; there must be the push for a radical and total change.

It is not by taking a mere mental attitude that this can be done or even by any number of inner experiences which leave the outer man as he was. It is this outer man who has to open, to surrender and to change. His every least movement, habit, action has to be surrendered, seen, held up and exposed to the divine Light, offered to the divine Force for its old forms and motives to be destroyed and the divine Truth and the action of the transforming consciousness of the Divine Mother to take their place.

*

There is not much spiritual meaning in keeping open to the Mother if you withhold your surrender. Self-giving or surrender is demanded of those who practise this

Yoga, because without such a progressive surrender of the being it is quite impossible to get anywhere near the goal. To keep open means to call in her Force to work in you, and if you do not surrender to it, it amounts to not allowing the Force to work in you at all or else only on condition that it will work in the way you want and not in its own way which is the way of the Divine Truth. A suggestion of this kind is usually made by some adverse Power or by some egoistic element of mind or vital which wants the Grace or the Force, but only in order to use it for its own purpose, and is not willing to live for the Divine Purpose, – it is willing to take from the Divine all it can get, but not to give itself to the Divine. The soul, the true being, on the contrary, turns towards the Divine and is not only willing but eager and happy to surrender.

In this Yoga one is supposed to go beyond every mental idealistic culture. Ideas and Ideals belong to the mind and are half-truths only; the mind too is, more often than not, satisfied with merely having an ideal, with the pleasure of idealising, while life remains always the same, untransformed or changed only a little and mostly in appearance. The spiritual seeker does not turn aside from the pursuit of realisation to mere idealising; not to idealise, but to realise the Divine Truth is always his aim, either beyond or in life also – and in the latter case it is necessary to transform mind and life which cannot be done without surrender to the action of the Divine Force, the Mother.

To seek after the Impersonal is the way of those who want to withdraw from life, and usually they try by their

own effort, and not by an opening of themselves to a superior Power or by the way of surrender; for the Impersonal is not something that guides or helps, but something to be attained and it leaves each man to attain it according to the way and capacity of his nature. On the other hand, by an opening and surrender to the Mother one can realise the Impersonal and every other aspect of Truth also.

The surrender must necessarily be progressive. No one can make the complete surrender from the beginning, so it is quite natural that when one looks into oneself, one should find its absence. That is no reason why the principle of surrender should not be accepted and carried out steadily from stage to stage, from field to field, applying it successively to all the parts of the nature.

*

In the early part of the Sadhana – and by early I do not mean a short part – effort is indispensable. Surrender of course, but surrender is not a thing that is done in a day. The mind has its ideas and it clings to them; the human vital resists surrender, for what it calls surrender in the early stages is a doubtful kind of self-giving with a demand in it; the physical consciousness is like a stone and what it calls surrender is often no more than inertia. It is only the psychic that knows how to surrender and the psychic is usually very much veiled in the beginning. When the psychic awakes, it can bring a sudden and true surrender of the whole being, for the difficulty of the

rest is rapidly dealt with and disappears. But till then effort is indispensable. Or else it is necessary till the Force comes flooding down into the being from above and takes up the Sadhana, does it for one more and more and leaves less and less to individual effort – but even then, if not effort, at least aspiration and vigilance are needed till the possession of mind, will, life and body by the Divine Power is complete. I have dealt with this subject, I think, in one of the chapters of "The Mother".

On the other hand, there are some people who start with a genuine and dynamic will for a total surrender. It is those who are governed by the psychic or are governed by a clear and enlightened mental will which, having once accepted surrender as the law of the Sadhana, will stand no nonsense about it and insists on the other parts of the being following its direction. Here there is still effort; but it is so ready and spontaneous and has so much the sense of a greater Force behind it that the Sadhak hardly feels that he is making an effort at all. In the contrary case of a will in mind or vital to retain self-will, a reluctance to give up your independent movement, there must be struggle and endeavour until the wall between the instrument in front and the Divinity behind or above is broken. No rule can be laid down which applies without distinction to everybody – the variations in human nature are too great to be covered by a single trenchant rule.

*

There is a state in which the Sadhak is conscious of

the Divine Force working in him or of its results at least and does not obstruct its descent or its action by his own mental activities, vital restlessness or physical obscurity and inertia. That is openness to the Divine. Surrender is the best way of opening; but aspiration and quietness can do it up to a certain point so long as there is not the surrender. Surrender means to consecrate everything in oneself to the Divine, to offer all one is and has, not to insist on one's ideas, desires, habits, etc., but to allow the divine Truth to replace them by its knowledge, will and action everywhere.

*

Always keep in touch with the Divine Force. The best thing for you is to do that simply and allow it to do its own work; wherever necessary, it will take hold of the inferior energies and purify them; at other times it will empty you of them and fill you with itself. But if you let your mind take the lead and discuss and decide what is to be done, you will lose touch with the Divine Force and the lower energies will begin to act for themselves and all go into confusion and a wrong movement.

*

Then only can the psychic being fully open when the Sadhak has got rid of the mixture of vital motives with his Sadhana and is capable of a simple and sincere self-offering to the Mother. If there is any kind of egoistic turn or insincerity of motive, if the Yoga is done under a pressure of vital demands, or partly or wholly to satisfy

some spiritual or other ambition, pride, vanity or seeking after power, position or influence over others or with any push towards satisfying any vital desire with the help of the Yogic force, then the psychic cannot open, or opens only partially or only at times and shuts again because it is veiled by the vital activities; the psychic fire fails in the strangling vital smoke. Also, if the mind takes the leading part in the Yoga and puts the inner soul into the background, or if the Bhakti or other movements of the Sadhana take more of a vital than of a psychic form, there is the same inability. Purity, simple sincerity and the capacity of an unegoistic unmixed self-offering without pretension or demand are the conditions of an entire opening of the psychic being.

*

It is no part of this Yoga to dry up the heart; but the emotions must be turned towards the Divine. There may be short periods in which the heart is quiescent, turned away from the ordinary feelings and waiting for the inflow from above; but such states are not states of dryness but of silence and peace. The heart in this Yoga should in fact be the main centre of concentration until the consciousness rises above.

*

All attachment is a hindrance to Sadhana. Goodwill you should have for all, psychic kindness for all, but no vital attachment.

*

The love of the Sadhak should be for the Divine. It is only when he has that fully that he can love others in the right way.

*

There is no reason why one should not receive through the thinking mind, as one receives through the vital, the emotional and the body. The thinking mind is as capable of receiving as these are, and, since it has to be transformed as well as the rest, it must be trained to receive, otherwise no transformation of it could take place.

It is the ordinary unenlightened activity of the intellect that is an obstacle to spiritual experience, just as the ordinary unregenerated activity of the vital or the obscure stupidly obstructive consciousness of the body is an obstacle. What the Sadhak has to be specially warned against in the wrong processes of the intellect is, first, any mistaking of mental ideas and impressions or intellectual conclusions for realisation; secondly, the restless activity of the mere mind which disturbs the spontaneous accuracy of psychic and spiritual experience and gives no room for the descent of the true illuminating knowledge or else deforms it as soon as it touches or even before it fully touches the human mental plane. There are also of course the usual vices of the intellect, – its leaning towards sterile doubt instead of luminous reception and calm enlightened discrimination; its arrogance claiming to judge things that are beyond it, unknown to it, too deep for it by standards drawn from its own limited experience; its attempts to explain the supraphysical by

the physical or its demand for the proof of higher and occult things by the criteria proper to Matter and mind in Matter; others also too many to enumerate here. Always it is substituting its own representations and constructions and opinions for the true knowledge. But if the intellect is surrendred, open, quiet, receptive, there is no reason why it should not be a means of reception of the Light or an aid to the experience of spiritual states and to the fullness of an inner change.

*

The turmoil of mental (intellectual) activity has also to be silenced like the vital activity of desire in order that the calm and peace may be complete. Knowledge has to come but from above. In this calm the ordinary mental activities like the ordinary vital activities become surface movements with which the silent inner self is not connected. It is the liberation necessary in order that the true knowledge and the true life-activity may replace or transform the activities of the Ignorance.

*

The soul, the psychic being is in direct touch with the divine Truth, but it is hidden in man by the mind, the vital being and the physical nature. One may practise Yoga and get illuminations in the mind and the reason; one may conquer power and luxuriate in all kinds of experiences in the vital; one may establish even surprising physical Siddhis; but if the true soul-power behind does not manifest, if the psychic nature does not come into

the front, nothing genuine has been done. In this Yoga the psychic being is that which opens the rest of the nature to the true supramental light and finally to the supreme Ananda. Mind can open by itself to its own higher reaches; it can still itself and widen into the Impersonal; it may too spiritualise itself in some kind of static liberation or Nirvana; but the Supramental cannot find a sufficient base in a spiritualised mind alone. If the inmost soul is awakened, if there is a new birth out of the mere mental, vital and physical into the psychic consciousness, then this Yoga can be done; otherwise (by the sole power of the mind or any other part) it is impossible.... If there is a refusal of the psychic new birth, a refusal to become the child new born from the Mother, owing to attachment to intellectual knowledge or mental ideas or to some vital desire, then there will be a failure in the Sadhana.

*

I have said that the most decisive way for the Peace or the Silence to come is by a descent from above. In fact, in reality though not always in appearance, that is how they always come; – not in appearance always, because the Sadhak is not always conscious of the process; he feels the peace settling in him or at least manifesting, but he has not been conscious how and whence it came. Yet it is the truth that all that belongs to the higher consciousness comes from above, not only the spiritual peace and silence, but the Light, the Power, the Knowledge, the higher seeing and thought, the Ananda come from above.

It is also possible that up to a certain point they may come from within, but this is because the psychic being is open to them directly and they come first there and then reveal themselves in the rest of the being from the psychic or by its coming into the front. A disclosure from within or a descent from above, these are the two sovereign ways of the Yoga-Siddhi. An effort of the external surface mind or emotions, a Tapasya of some kind may seem to build up some of these things, but the results are usually uncertain and fragmentary, compared to the result of the two radical ways. That is why in this Yoga we insist always on an "opening" – an opening inwards of the inner mind, vital, physical to the inmost part of us, the psychic, and an opening upwards to what is above the mind – as indispensable for the fruits of the Sadhana.

The underlying reason for this is that this little mind, vital and body which we call ourselves is only a surface movement and not our "self" at all. It is an external bit of personality put forward for one brief life, for the play of the Ignorance. It is equipped with an ignorant mind stumbling about in search of fragments of truth, an ignorant vital rushing about in search of fragments of pleasure, an obscure and mostly subconscious physical receiving the impacts of things and suffering rather than possessing a resultant pain or pleasure. All that is accepted until the mind gets disgusted and starts looking about for the real Truth of itself and things, the vital gets disgusted and begins wondering whether there is not such a thing as real bliss and the physical gets tired and wants libera-

tion from itself and its pains and pleasures. Then it is possible for the little ignorant bit of personality to get back to its real Self and with it to these greater things – or else to extinction of itself, Nirvana.

The real Self is not anywhere on the surface but deep within and above. Within is the soul supporting an inner mind, inner vital, inner physical in which there is a capacity for universal wideness and with it for the things now asked for – direct contact with the truth of self and things, taste of a universal bliss, liberation from the imprisoned smallness and sufferings of the gross physical body. Even in Europe the existence of something behind the surface is now very frequently admitted, but its nature is mistaken and it is called subconscient or subliminal, while really it is very conscious in its own way and not subliminal but only behind the veil. It is, according to our psychology, connected with the small outer personality by certain centres of consciousness of which we become aware by Yoga. Only a little of the inner being escapes through these centres into the outer life, but that little is the best part of ourselves and responsible for our art, poetry, philosophy, ideals, religious aspirations, efforts at knowledge and perfection. But the inner centres are for the most part closed or asleep – to open them and make them awake and active is one aim of Yoga. As they open, the powers and possibilities of the inner being also are aroused in us; we awake first to a larger consciousness and then to a cosmic consciousness; we are no longer little separate personalities with limited lives but centres of a universal action and in direct contact with cosmic

forces. Moreover, instead of being unwillingly playthings of the latter, as is the surface person, we can become to a certain extent conscious and masters of the play of nature – how far this goes depending on the development of the inner being and its opening upward to the higher spiritual levels. At the same time the opening of the heart centre releases the psychic being which proceeds to make us aware of the Divine within us and of the higher Truth above us.

For the highest spiritual Self is not even behind our personality and bodily existence but is above it and altogether exceeds it. The highest of the inner centres is in the head, just as the deepest is the heart; but the centre which opens directly to the Self is above the head, altogether outside the physical body, in what is called the subtle body, *sūkṣma śarīra.* This Self has two aspects and the results of realising it correspond to these two aspects. One is static, a condition of wide peace, freedom, silence: the silent Self is unaffected by any action or experience; it impartially supports them but does not seem to originate them at all, rather to stand back detached or unconcerned, *udāsīna.* The other aspect is dynamic and that is experienced as a cosmic Self or Spirit which not only supports but originates and contains the whole cosmic action – not only that part of it which concerns our physical selves but also all that is beyond it – this world and all other worlds, the supraphysical as well as the physical ranges of the universe. Moreover, we feel the Self as one in all; but also we feel it as above all, transcendent, surpassing all individual birth or cosmic exist-

ence. To get into the universal Self – one in all – is to be liberated from ego; ego either becomes a small instrumental circumstance in the consciousness or even disappears from our consciousness altogether. That is the extinction or Nirvana of the ego. To get into the transcendent self above all makes us capable of transcending altogether even cosmic consciousness and action – it can be the way to that complete liberation from the world-existence which is called also extinction, *laya, mokṣa, nirvāna.*

It must be noted however that the opening upward does not necessarily lead to peace, silence and Nirvana only. The Sadhak becomes aware not only of a great, eventually an infinite peace, silence, wideness above us, above the head as it were and extending into all physical and supra-physical space, but also he can become aware of other things – a vast Force in which is all power, a vast Light in which is all knowledge, a vast Ananda in which is all bliss and rapture. At first they appear as something essential, indeterminate, absolute, simple, *kevala*: a Nirvana into any of these things seems possible. But we can come to see too that this Force contains all forces, this Light all lights, this Ananda all joy and bliss possible. And all this can descend into us. Any of them and all of them can come down, not peace alone; only the safest is to bring down first an absolute calm and peace, for that makes the descent of the rest more secure; otherwise it may be difficult for the external nature to contain or bear so much Force, Light, Knowledge or Ananda. All these things together make what we call the higher

spiritual or Divine Consciousness. The psychic opening through the heart puts us primarily into connection with the individual Divine, the Divine in his inner relation with us; it is especially the source of love and Bhakti. This upward opening puts us into direct relation with the whole Divine and can create in us the divine consciousness and a new birth or births of the spirit.

When the Peace is established, this higher or Divine Force from above can descend and work in us. It descends usually first into the head and liberates the inner mind centres, then into the heart centre and liberates fully the psychic and emotional being, then into the navel and other vital centres and liberates the inner vital, then into the Muladhara and below and liberates the inner physical being. It works at the same time for perfection as well as liberation; it takes up the whole nature part by part and deals with it, rejecting what has to be rejected, sublimating what has to be sublimated, creating what has to be created. It integrates, harmonises, establishes a new rhythm in the nature. It can bring down too a higher and yet higher force and range of the higher nature until, if that be the aim of the Sadhana, it becomes possible to bring down the supramental force and existence. All this is prepared, assisted, farthered by the work of the psychic being in the heart centre; the more it is open, in front, active, the quicker, safer, easier the working of the Force can be. The more love and Bhakti and surrender grow in the heart, the more rapid and perfect becomes the evolution of the Sadhana. For the descent and transformation imply at the same time an increasing contact

and union with the Divine.

That is the fundamental rationale of the Sadhana. It will be evident that the two most important things here are the opening of the heart centre and the opening of the mind centres to all that is behind and above them. For the heart opens to the psychic being and the mind centres open to the higher consciousness and the nexus between the psychic being and the higher consciousness is the principal means of the Siddhi. The first opening is effected by a concentration in the heart, a call to the Divine to manifest within us and through the psychic to take up and lead the whole nature. Aspiration, prayer, Bhakti, love, surrender are the main supports of this part of the Sadhana – accompanied by a rejection of all that stands in the way of what we aspire for. The second opening is effected by a concentration of the consciousness in the head (afterwards, above it) and an aspiration and call and a sustained will for the descent of the divine Peace, Power, Light, Knowledge, Ananda into the being – the Peace first or the Peace and Force together. Some indeed receive Light first or Ananda first or some sudden pouring down of Knowledge. With some there is first an opening which reveals to them a vast infinite Silence, Force, Light or Bliss above them and afterwards either they ascend to that or these things begin to descend into the lower nature. With others there is either the descent, first into the head, then down to the heart level, then to the navel and below and through the whole body, or else an inexplicable opening – without any sense of descent – of peace, light, wideness or power, or else a hori-

zontal opening into the cosmic consciousness or in a suddenly widened mind an outburst of knowledge. Whatever comes has to be welcomed – for there is no absolute rule for all – but if the peace has not come first, care must be taken not to swell oneself in exultation or lose the balance. The capital movement however is when the Divine Force or Shakti, the power of the Mother comes down and takes hold, for then the organisation of the consciousness begins and the larger foundation of the Yoga.

The result of the concentration is not usually immediate – though to some there comes a swift and sudden outflowering; but with most there is a time longer or shorter of adaptation or preparation, especially if the nature has not been prepared already to some extent by aspiration and Tapasya. The coming of the result can sometimes be aided by associating with the concentration one of the processes of the old Yoga. There is the Adwaita process of the way of knowledge – one rejects from oneself the identification with the mind, vital, body, saying continually "I am not the mind", "I am not the vital", "I am not the body", seeing these things as separate from one's real self – and after a time one feels all the mental, vital, physical processes and the very sense of mind, vital, body becoming externalised, an outer action, while within and detached from them there grows the sense of a separate self-existent being which opens into the realisation of the cosmic and transcendent spirit. There is also the method – a very powerful method – of the Sankhyas, the separation of the Purusha and the

Prakriti. One enforces on the mind the position of the Witness – all action of mind, vital, physical becomes an outer play which is not myself or mine, but belongs to Nature and has been enforced on an outer me. I am the witness Purusha; I am silent, detached, not bound by any of these things. There grows up in consequence a division in the being; the Sadhak feels within him the growth of a calm silent separate consciousness which feels itself quite apart from the surface play of the mind and the vital and physical Nature. Usually when this takes place, it is possible very rapidly to bring down the peace of the higher consciousness and the action of the higher Force and the full march of the Yoga. But often the Force itself comes down first in response to the concentration and call and then, if these things are necessary, it does them and uses any other means or process that is helpful or indispensable.

One thing more. In this process of the descent from above and the working it is most important not to rely entirely on oneself, but to rely on the guidance of the Guru and to refer all that happens to his judgment and arbitration and decision. For it often happens that the forces of the lower nature are stimulated and excited by the descent and want to mix with it and turn it to their profit. It often happens too that some Power or Powers undivine in their nature present themselves as the Supreme Lord or as the Divine Mother and claim the being's service and surrender. If these things are accepted, there will be an extremely disastrous consequence. If indeed there is the assent of the Sadhak to the Divine working alone

and the submission or surrender to that guidance, then all can go smoothly. This assent and a rejection of all egoistic forces or forces that appeal to the ego are the safeguard throughout the Sadhana. But the ways of nature are full of snares, the disguises of the ego are innumerable, the illusions of the Powers of Darkness, Rakshasi Maya, are extraordinarily skilful; the reason is an insufficient guide and often turns traitor; vital desire is always with us tempting to follow any alluring call. This is the reason why in this Yoga we insist so much on what we call Samarpana – rather inadequately rendered by the English word surrender. If the heart centre is fully opened and the psychic is always in control, then there is no question; all is safe. But the psychic can at any moment be veiled by a lower upsurge. It is only a few who are exempt from these dangers and it is precisely those to whom surrender is easily possible. The guidance of one who himself is by identity or represents the Divine is in this difficult endeavour imperative and indispensable.

What I have written may help you to get some clear idea of what I mean by the central process of the Yoga. I have written at some length but, naturally, could cover only the fundamental things. Whatever belongs to circumstance and detail must arise as one works out the method, or rather as it works itself out – for the last is what usually happens when there is an effective beginning of the action of the Sadhana.

*

Then as to concentration. Ordinarily the conscious-

ness is spread out everywhere, dispersed, running in this or that direction, after this subject and that object in multitude. When anything has to be done of a sustained nature the first thing one does is to draw back all this dispersed consciousness and concentrate. It is then, if one looks closely, bound to be concentrated in one place and on one occupation, subject or object – as when you are composing a poem or a botanist is studying a flower. The place is usually somewhere in the brain if it is the thought, in the heart if it is the feeling in which one is concentrated. The Yogic concentration is simply an extension and intensification of the same thing. It may be on an object as when one does Tratak on a shining point – then one has to concentrate so that one sees only that point and has no other thought than that. It may be on an idea or word or a name, the idea of the Divine, the word OM, the name Krishna, or a combination of idea and word or idea and name. But further in Yoga one also concentrates in a particular place. There is the famous rule of concentrating between the eyebrows – the centre of the inner mind, of occult vision, of the will is there. What you do is to think firmly from there on whatever you make the object of your concentration or else try to see the image of it from there. If you succeed in this then after a time you feel that your whole consciousness is centred there in that place – of course for the time being. After doing it for some time and often it beomes easy and normal.

I hope this is clear. Well, in this Yoga, you do the same, not necessarily at that particular spot between the

eyebrows, but anywhere in the head or at the centre of the chest where the physiologists have fixed the cardiac centre. Instead of concentrating on an object, you concentrate in the head in a will, a call for the descent of the peace above or, as some do, an opening of the unseen lid and an ascent of the consciousness above. In the heart centre one concentrates in an aspiration, for an opening, for the presence of the living image of the Divine there or whatever else is the object. There may be Japa of a name but, if so, there must also be a concentration on it and the name must repeat itself there in the heart centre.

It may be asked what becomes of the rest of the consciousness when there is this local concentration? Well, it either falls silent as in any concentration or, if it does not, then thoughts or other things may move about, as if outside, but the concentrated part does not attend to them or notice. That is when the concentration is reasonably successful.

One has not to fatigue oneself at first by long concentration if one is not accustomed, for then in a jaded mind it loses its power and value. One can relax and meditate instead of concentrating. It is only as the concentration becomes normal that one can go on for a longer and longer time.

WORK

To go entirely inside in order to have experiences and to neglect the work, the external consciousness, is to be unbalanced, one-sided in the Sadhana – for our Yoga is integral; so also to throw oneself outward and live in the external being alone is to be unbalanced, one-sided in the Sadhana. One must have the same consciousness in inner experience and outward action and make both full of the Mother.

*

To keep up work helps to keep up the balance between the internal experience and the external development; otherwise one-sidedness and want of measure and balance may develop. Moreover, it is necessary to keep the Sadhana of work for the Divine because in the end that enables the Sadhak to bring out the inner progress into the external nature and life and helps the integrality of the Sadhana.

*

Everything depends on the inner condition, and the outward condition is only useful as a means and a help for expressing or confirming the inner condition and making it dynamic and effective. If you do or say a thing with the psychic uppermost or with the right inner touch, it will be effective; if you do or say the same thing out of the mind or the vital or with a wrong or mixed atmosphere, it may be quite ineffective. To do the right thing

in the right way in each case and at each moment one must be in the right consciousness – it cannot be done by following a fixed mental rule which under some circumstances might fit in and under others might not fit at all. A general principle can be laid down if it is in consonance with the Truth, but its application must be determined by the inner consciousness seeing at each step what is to be done and not done. If the psychic is uppermost, if the being is entirely turned towards the Mother and follows the psychic, this can be increasingly done.

*

There should be not only a general attitude, but each work should be offered to the Mother so as to keep the attitude a living one all the time. There should be at the time of work no meditation, for that would withdraw the attention from the work, but there should be the constant memory of the One to whom you offer it. This is only a first process; for when you can have constantly the feeling of a calm being within concentrated in the sense of the Divine Presence while the surface mind does the work, or when you can begin to feel always that it is the Mother's force that is doing the work and you are only a channel or an instrument, then in place of memory there will have begun the automatic constant realisation of Yoga, divine union, in works.

*

The only work that spiritually purifies is that which is done without personal motives, without desire for fame

or public recognition or worldly greatness, without insistence on one's own mental motives or vital lusts and demands or physical preferences, without vanity or crude self-assertion or claim for position or prestige, done for the sake of the Divine alone and at the command of the Divine. All work done in an egoistic spirit, however good for people in the world of the Ignorance, is of no avail to the seeker of the Yoga.

*

The ordinary life consists in work for personal aim and satisfaction of desire under some mental or moral control, touched sometimes by a mental ideal. The Gita's Yoga consists in the offering of one's work as a sacrifice to the Divine, the conquest of desire, egoless and desireless action, Bhakti for the Divine, an entering into the cosmic consciousness, the sense of unity with all creatures, oneness with the Divine. This Yoga adds the bringing down of the supramental Light and Force (its ultimate aim) and the transformation of the nature.

*

Self-dedication does not depend on the particular work you do, but on the spirit in which all work, of whatever kind it may be, is done. Any work done well and carefully as a sacrifice to the Divine, without desire or egoism, with equality of mind and calm tranquillity in good or bad fortune, for the sake of the Divine and not for the sake of any personal gain, reward or result, with the consciousness that it is the Divine Power to

which all work belongs, is a means of self-dedication through Karma.

*

Even the most purely physical and mechanical work cannot be properly done if one accepts incapacity, inertia and passivity. The remedy is not to confine yourself to mechanical work, but to reject and throw off incapacity, passivity and inertia and open yourself to the Mother's force. If vanity, ambition and self-conceit stand in your way, cast them from you. You will not get rid of these things by merely waiting for them to disappear. If you merely wait for things to happen, there is no reason why they should happen at all. If it is incapacity and weakness that oppose, still, as one opens oneself truly and more and more to the Mother's force, the strength and capacity necessary for the work will be given and will grow in the Adhar.

*

Those who do work for the Mother in all sincerity are prepared by the work itself for the right consciousness even if they do not sit down for meditation or follow any particular practice of Yoga. It is not necessary to tell you how to meditate; whatever is needful will come of itself if in your work and at all times you are sincere and keep yourself open to the Mother.

*

Openness in work means the same thing as openness

in the consciousness. The same Force that works in your consciousness in meditation and clears away the cloud and confusion whenever you open to it, can also take up your action and not only make you aware of the defects in it but keep you conscious of what is to be done and guide your mind and hands to do it. If you open to it in your work, you will begin to feel this guidance more and more until behind all your activities you will be aware of the Force of the Mother.

*

There is no stage of the Sadhana in which works are impossible, no passage in the path where there is no foothold and action has to be renounced as incompatible with concentration on the Divine. The foothold is there always; the foothold is the reliance on the Divine, the opening of the being, the will, the energies to the Divine, the surrender to the Divine. All work done in that spirit can be made a means for the Sadhana. It may be necessary for an individual here and there to plunge into meditation for a time and suspend work for that time or make it subordinate; but that can only be an individual case and a temporary retirement. Moreover, a complete cessation of work and entire withdrawal into oneself is seldom advisable; it may encourage a too one-sided and visionary condition in which one lives in a sort of midworld of purely subjective experiences without a firm hold on either external reality or on the highest Reality and without the right use of the subjective experience to create a firm link and then a unification between the

highest Reality and the external realisation in life.

Work can be of two kinds – the work that is a field of experience used for the Sadhana, for a progressive harmonisation and transformation of the being and its activities, and work that is a realised expression of the Divine. But the time for the latter can be only when the Realisation has been fully brought down into the earth-consciousness; till then all work must be a field of endeavour and a school of experience.

*

I have never put any ban on Bhakti. Also I am not conscious of having banned meditation either at any time. I have stressed both Bhakti and knowledge in my Yoga as well as works, even if I have not given any of them an exclusive importance like Shankara or Chaitanya.

The difficulty you feel or any Sadhak feels about Sadhana is not really a question of meditation versus Bhakti versus works. It is a difficulty of the attitude to be taken, the approach or whatever you may like to call it.

If you can't as yet remember the Divine all the time you are working, it does not greatly matter. To remember and dedicate at the beginning and give thanks at the end ought to be enough for the present. Or at the most to remember too when there is a pause. Your method seems to me rather painful and difficult, – you seem to be trying to remember and work with one and the same part of the mind. I don't know if that is possible. When people remember all the time during work (it can be done), it is usually with the back of their minds or else

there is created gradually a faculty of double thought or else a double consciousness – one in front that works, and one within that witnesses and remembers. There is also another way which was mine for a long time – a condition in which the work takes place automatically and without intervention of personal thought or mental action, while the consciousness remains silent in the Divine. The thing, however, does not come so much by trying as by a very simple constant aspiration and will of consecration – or else by a movement of the consciousness separating the inner from the instrumental being. Aspiration and will of consecration calling down a greater Force to do the work is a method which brings great results, even if in some it takes a long time about it. That is a great secret of Sadhana, to know how to get things done by the Power behind or above instead of doing all by the mind's effort. I don't mean to say that the mind's effort is unnecessary or has no result – only if it tries to do everything by itself, that becomes a laborious effort for all except the spiritual athletes. Nor do I mean that the other method is the longed-for short cut; the result may, as I have said, take a long time. Patience and firm resolution are necessary in every method of Sadhana.

Strength is all right for the strong – but aspiration and the Grace answering to it are not altogether myths; they are great realities of the spiritual life.

*

I do not mean by work action done in the ego and the ignorance, for the satisfaction of the ego and in the

drive of Rajasic desire. There can be no Karmayoga without the will to get rid of ego, Rajas and desire, which are the seals of ignorance.

I do not mean philanthropy or the service of humanity or all the rest of the things – moral or idealistic – which the mind of man substitutes for the deeper truth of works.

I mean by work action done for the Divine and more and more in union with the Divine – for the Divine alone and nothing else. Naturally that is not easy at the beginning, any more than deep meditation and luminous Knowledge are easy or even true love and Bhakti are easy. But like the others it has to be begun in the right spirit and attitude, with the right will in you, then all the rest will come.

Works done in this spirit are quite as effective as Bhakti or contemplation. One gets by the rejection of desire, Rajas, and ego a quietude and purity into which the Peace ineffable can descend; one gets by the dedication of one's will to the Divine, by the merging of one's will in the Divine Will the death of ego and the enlarging into the cosmic consciousness or else the uplifting into what is above the cosmic; one experiences the separation of Purusha from Prakriti and is liberated from the shackles of the outer nature; one becomes aware of one's inner being and sees the outer as an instrument; one feels the universal Force doing one's works and the Self or Purusha watching or witness but free; one feels all one's works taken from one and done by the universal or supreme Mother or by the Divine Power controlling and acting

from behind the heart. By constant referring of all one's will and works to the Divine, love and adoration grow, the psychic being comes forward. By the reference to the Power above, we can come to feel it above and its descent and the opening to an increasing consciousness and knowledge. Finally, works, Bhakti and knowledge go together and self-perfection becomes possible – what we call the transformation of the nature.

These results certainly do not come all at once; they come more or less slowly, more or less completely according to the condition and growth of the being. There is no royal road to the divine realisation.

This is the Karmayoga laid down in the Gita as I have developed it for the integral spiritual life. It is founded not on speculation and reasoning but on experience. It does not exclude meditation and certainly does not exclude Bhakti, for the self-offering to the Divine, the consecration of all oneself to the Divine which is the essence of this Karmayoga are essentially a movement of Bhakti. Only it does exclude a life-fleeing exclusive meditation or an emotional Bhakti shut up in its own inner dream taken as the whole movement of the Yoga. One may have hours of pure absorbed meditation or of the inner motionless adoration and ecstasy, but they are not the whole of the integral Yoga.

GLOSSARY

ādhāra (Adhar): Vessel, receptacle – the system of mind, life and body considered as a receptacle of the spiritual consciousness and force.

advaita (Adwaita): Monism, monistic.

advaita vedānta (Adwaita Vedanta): The monistic school of Vedanta.

ājñā cakra: Will centre – see *cakra.*

anāhata: See *cakra.*

ānanda (Ananda): Bliss, delight – the divine or spiritual bliss.

antarātman (Antaratman): Inner self, soul.

aparā prakṛti (Apara Prakriti): The inferior nature, Nature in the lower manifestation of the Ignorance.

ātman (Atman): Self.

ātmarati: The peace and joy inherent in the self.

avatāra (Avatar): The descent of the Divine in a human form.

avidyā (Avidya): The cosmic principle of Ignorance.

bhakta: Devotee.

bhakti: Devotion.

brahman: The spiritual Reality, universal and supreme.

brahmāṇḍa (Brahmanda): Cosmos, universe.

caitya puruṣa (Chaitya Purusha): Psychic being.

cakra (Chakra): Centre, nodus, plexus; the seven psychological centres in the subtle body.

cakra, ājñā: Centre between the eye-brows.

—*anāhata*: Centre in the heart.
—*hṛdpadma*: Heart-lotus; same as *anāhata*.
—*maṇipura*: Centre at the navel.
—*mūlādhāra*: Centre at the bottom end of the spine.
—*nābhipadma*: Same as *manipura*.
—*sahasradala*: See *sahasradala*.
—*svādhiṣṭhāna*: Centre abdominal.
—*viśuddha*: Centre in the throat.

dvaita (Dwaita): Dualism, dualistic.
dvaitādvaita (Dwaitadwaita): Dualistic monism.

guṇa (Guna): Quality, mode of Nature.
guru: Spiritual Master.

hṛdpadma: See *cakra*.

japa: Repetition of set sounds or words or a name as prayer or invocation.
jīva (Jiva): The Jivatman; the living being.
jīva, Kṛṣṇa's (Jiva, Krishna's): A creature of Krishna, i.e., God's creature.
jīvātman (Jivatman): The individual self.
jyoti: Light; the principle of spiritual light in the higher or divine Nature.

karma: Action, work: the resultant force of action done in the past, especially in past lives.
karma Yoga: The system of spiritual discipline which takes work (dedicated to the Divine) as its basis.

kevala: Absolute, sheer.
kṛṣṇa's jīva (Krishna's Jiva): See *jīva, Kṛṣṇa's.*
kuṇḍalinī śakti (Kundalini Shakti): The power that lies coiled or involved in the lowest centre at the bottom of the spine; it is awakened by Yoga and rises to join the Divine Power or Presence in the 'sahasradala' (seventh centre).

laya: Dissolution of the individual being, merging in the one Self-Existence.
līlā (Lila): Play (of the Divine).

maṇipura: See *cakra.*
mantra: Set words or sounds having a spiritual significance and power.
mokṣa (Moksha): Spiritual liberation from the sense of personal being; release from cosmic existence.
mūlādhāra: See *cakra.*

nābhipadma: See *cakra.*
nirvāṇa (Nirvana): Spiritual extinction of the separate individual self.
om: The primal sound representing the supreme spiritual reality.

Parameśvara (Parameshwara): The Supreme as Lord and Master of the universe.
parā prakṛti: The higher or divine Nature.
parā prakṛtir jīvabhūtā: The higher Nature that has become the individual selves.
prakṛti (Prakriti): Nature, the active and executive Energy,

as distinguished from the witnessing and sustaining soul or conscious being.

pralaya: The dissolution of the cosmos; any dissolution of the created things.

puruṣa (Purusha): The soul or conscious being supporting the action of Nature.

rajas: One of the three gunas, fundamental qualities or modes of Nature; the kinetic principle in Nature characterised by desire, action and passions.

rājasika (Rajasic): Full of the quality of *rajas*, the kinetic principle.

rākṣasī māyā (Rakshasi Maya): Illusions created by the Powers of Darkness.

śakti (Shakti): The Divine Power, the Conscious Force of the Divine.

śama (Shama): Quiet, rest – the principle of calm and peace in the higher or divine Nature.

śrāddha (Shraddha): The ceremony of offering oblation to the dead.

saccidānanda (Sachchidananda): The Supreme Reality as self-existent Being, Consciousness and Bliss.

sahasradala: The thousand-petalled lotus, seventh centre at the crown of the head.

samarpaṇa (Samarpana): Entire self-giving, surrender, dedication.

saṁskāras (Sanskaras): Fixed mental formations; impressions of past habits, experiences stored up in the subconscious parts.

sattva (Sattwa): One of the three gunas, fundamental qualities or modes of Nature; the principle of light and harmony in Nature.

sādhaka (Sadhak): One who practises the discipline of Yoga.

sādhanā (Sadhana): The discipline of Yoga as a means of realisation; practice of the Yoga.

sāṁkhya (Sankhya): A system of philosophy and spiritual practice based upon a detailed analysis of nature and consciousness, Prakriti and Purusha.

Sāttvika (Sattwic): Full of the quality of *sattva,* the principle of light and harmony.

siddhi: Realisation, fulfilment; also, an occult power gained by Yoga.

sūkṣma śarīra (Sukshma Sharira): The subtle body.

svādhiṣṭhāna: See *cakra.*

tamas: One of the three gunas, fundamental qualities or modes of Nature; the principle of obscurity and inertia in Nature.

tantra: A path of spiritual discipline based upon the principle of Consciousness-Power (conceived as the Mother) as the supreme Reality.

tapas: Energy of Consciousness – the principle of spiritual power and force in the higher or divine Nature.

tapasyā (Tapasya): Spiritual effort by concentration of the energies in a spiritual discipline or process.

tāmasika (Tamasic): Full of the quality of *tamas*, the principle of obscurity and inertia in Nature.

trāṭaka (Tratak): Focussing the eyes upon a single point

to make the consciousness one-pointed.

udāsīna (Udasina): Seated above, detached.

vedānta (Vedanta): The system of philosophy and spiritual discipline in accordance with the "Book of Knowledge" that forms the latter portion of the Vedas (the Vedas are the ancient Indian Scriptures) – the earlier portion being known as the "Book of Works".

viśuddha: Literally, pure, see *cakra*.

viśiṣṭādvaita (Vishishtadwaita): Qualified monism.

vṛndāvana (Vrindavan): The holy place where Krishna as the Divine Lover plays with his beloved ones.

yoga: Union with the Divine; the discipline by which one enters through an awakening into an inner and higher consciousness.

yoga-śakti (Yoga-Shakti): The power that comes with the awakening of the inner and higher consciousness.

yoga siddhi: Fulfilment or realisation of the aims of the Yoga.